"Got a problem? Need a practical, innovative sol[ution to] implement tomorrow? Look no further. In *Hacking Education*, Mark Barnes and Jennifer Gonzalez combine decades of teaching experience with hacker ingenuity, mixing a nifty recipe for success in any school. *Hacking Education* is more than a how-to book for best practices in the classroom. It's a blueprint for finding more time in your day, creating a culture of readers, solving daily tech woes, building rapport with students, and turning chaos into peace. Barnes and Gonzalez don't just solve problems; they turn teachers into hackers—a transformation that is right on time."

— **DON WETTRICK**, AUTHOR OF *PURE GENIUS: BUILDING A CULTURE OF INNOVATION AND TAKING 20% TIME TO THE NEXT LEVEL*

"With *Hacking Education*, Mark and Jennifer have created something really powerful! By identifying current problems in education and proposing creative solutions, they're helping educators get past the obstacles that often impede progress, and instead focus in on what really counts: student learning."

— **PAUL SOLARZ**, AUTHOR OF *LEARN LIKE A PIRATE: EMPOWER YOUR STUDENTS TO COLLABORATE, LEAD, AND SUCCEED*

"There aren't many quick fixes in education. But Barnes and Gonzalez have identified 10 surprisingly doable ways to hack the status quo in schools. This highly readable book tackles problems that lead to teacher frustration (like long, pointless meetings and turning students into numbers) as well as goals that educators strive toward but often find tough to manage (such as flipping the learning and collaborating with other teachers). *Hacking Education* accurately describes the challenges schools are facing and provides creative, cutting edge, and easy-to-implement solutions that create a big impact in a short time period."

— **ANGELA WATSON**, AUTHOR OF *UNSHAKEABLE: 20 WAYS TO ENJOY TEACHING EVERY DAY...NO MATTER WHAT*

"Jennifer and Mark are two educators that know how to transform some of the most frustrating teacher problems into easy-to-implement solutions. Each hack in this book is presented in a clear and logical manner. I found myself agreeing over and over again with the sensibility of their ideas. Yet, as we all know, good ideas in education sometime get stopped in their tracks. Thankfully Jennifer and Mark have provided simple steps that anyone can take to overcome resistance and pushback against the doubters. *Hacking Education* proves that anyone— from a first year-teacher to a 30-year veteran—can be a more effective teacher and be a positive agent of change in their school's culture."

— **BRIAN SZTABNIK**, HOST OF THE *TALKS WITH TEACHERS* PODCAST AND WRITER AT EDUTOPIA

"*Hacking Education* is more than just a book for teachers and school leaders. Mark Barnes and Jennifer Gonzalez provide a simple blueprint for smart and efficient changes that every school can benefit from regardless of its current situation."

— **A.J. JULIANI**, AUTHOR OF *LEARNING BY CHOICE: 10 WAYS TO TRANSFORM YOUR CLASSROOM INTO A STUDENT-CENTERED EXPERIENCE*

"Insightful... Schools and teachers that want to go from good to great must read *Hacking Education*. You'll be delighted by how simple it is to apply these hacks into your workflow. Barnes and Gonzalez provide a refreshingly modern take on a system that has become old and sclerotic—our schools. Their writing is succinct; it resonates and smacks you with the deliverables."

— **DANIEL MCCABE**, ASSISTANT PRINCIPAL ACCOMPSETT MIDDLE SCHOOL, SMITHTOWN, NY

HACKING EDUCATION

HACKING EDUCATION

10 Quick Fixes for Every School

Mark Barnes
Jennifer Gonzalez

Hacking Education

© 2015 by Times 10 Publications

These books are available at special discounts when purchased in quantity for use as premiums, promotions, fundraising, and educational use. For inquiries and details, contact us: mark@times10books.com.

Published by Times 10 Publications
Cleveland, OH
http://hacklearningseries.com

Cover Design by Tracey Henterly

Interior Design by Steven Plummer

Editing by Georgina Chong-You

Library of Congress Control Number: 2015908743

ISBN: 978-0-9861049-0-9

First Times 10 Publications Printing

CONTENTS

ACKNOWLEDGEMENTS

WE'D LIKE TO thank the amazing people in the Talks With Teachers community, especially those in the TWT Voxer group. You inspired us to turn a discussion about problem solving into a book. Thanks Lisa Hubler, Joe Mazza, Starr Sackstein, Abby Morton, Barbara LaBarre, Roxie Oberg, Mark Levezow, Lisa Tremonte, Barry Sanders, and the tech-savvy students at Richardsville Elementary for your contributions.

Mark: I would like to thank my wife, Mollie, and my children, Ethan and Lauren, for their ongoing love and support. Thank you Dave Burgess for letting me pick your brain. Special thanks to the amazing Jennifer Gonzalez, the best Hacker I know.

Jennifer: I'm grateful to Mark Barnes for giving me such a great opportunity, for believing in this project, and for showing me what a true trailblazer looks like. A big thank you to my kids, Mia, Ruby, and Danny, for putting up with Mommy being on the computer so much. Finally, I want to thank my husband, Ralph, for thinking every idea I come up with is possible.

ABOUT THE HACK
LEARNING SERIES

"Hackers don't take realities of the world for granted;
they seek to break and rebuild what they don't like."
—SARAH LACY, AUTHOR/JOURNALIST

A HACKER IS SOMEONE who explores programmable systems and molds them into something different, often, something better. Hackers are known as computer geeks—people who like to take applications and algorithms to places their designers never intended. Today, hackers are much more. They are people who explore many things both in and out of the technology world. They are tinkerers and fixers. They see solutions to problems that other people do not see. Steve Jobs and Mark Zuckerberg might be considered technology's greatest hackers. No one taught them how to build an operating system or a social network, but they saw possibilities that others couldn't see.

The Hack Learning Series is a collection of books written by people who, like Jobs and Zuckerberg, see things through a different lens. They are teachers, researchers, and consultants; they are administrators, professors, and specialists. They live to solve problems whose solutions, in many cases, already exist but may need to be hacked. In other words, the problem needs to be turned upside down or viewed from another perspective. Its fix may appear unreasonable to those plagued by the issue. To the hacker, though, the solution is evident, and with a little hacking, it will be as clear and beautiful as a gracefully-designed smartphone or a powerful social network.

THE STORY BEHIND THE SERIES

In 2014, I had an idea about three problems in schools that I felt could be easily fixed. What they needed was the perspective of a hacker—someone unaffected by the problem, who viewed its underlying issues from a different angle. I wrote a short blog post identifying the problems and included very easy fixes. The post sparked plenty of thoughtful discussion, and someone suggested that schools have more concerns, similar to the ones in the blog post—enough, perhaps, for a book. Some time later, three school problems became 10. All they needed was space on a page and a hacker's finesse.

I began collaborating with a smart educator named Jennifer Gonzalez, and soon we had a table of contents and chapter outlines for 10 Hacks. Months later, we completed this book, the first in the Hack Learning Series. The quick fixes clear the path to better practice, open communication, and improved professional development. We believe that they can make schools wonderful places, even in a time when the bureaucracy makes education extremely difficult.

As we worked on developing our 10 hacks, we wondered about other learning issues that are not covered in *Hacking Education*. So many facets of learning need to be hacked: The Common Core, digital literacy, reluctant learners, special education, project-based learning, teacher preparation, assessment, leadership, and infrastructure, to name a few. When teachers, parents, administrators, and policymakers see the amazing insights that hackers can bring to various issues, they are sure to want more. Enter the *Hack Learning Series*—an evolving collection of books solving problems that impede learning in the world of education and beyond.

INSIDE THE BOOKS

Hack Learning books are written by passionate people who are experts in their fields. Unlike your typical education text, Hack Learning books are light on research and statistics and heavy on practical advice from people who have actually experienced the problems about which they write. Each book in the series contains chapters, called Hacks, which are composed of these sections:

- **The Problem:** Something educators are currently wrestling with that doesn't yet have a clear-cut solution.

- **The Hack**: A brief description of the prescribed solution.

- **What You Can Do Tomorrow:** Ways you can take the basic hack and implement it right away in bare-bones form.

- **Blueprint for Full Implementation:** A step-by-step system for building long-term capacity.

- **Overcoming Pushback:** A list of possible objections you might come up against in your attempt to implement this hack and how to overcome them.

- **The Hack in Action:** A snapshot of an educator or group of educators who have used this hack in their work and how they did it.

EDITOR'S PROMISE

I am so proud to be a contributing author and publisher of the Hack Learning Series, written by renowned educators, speakers, and thought leaders—all dedicated to improving teaching and learning. I promise that every Hack Learning book will provide powerful information, imagination, engaging prose, practical advice and maybe even a little humor. When you read a Hack Learning Series book, you'll have solutions you didn't have before.

MARK BARNES, AUTHOR/SPEAKER/HACKER

INTRODUCTION
A Hacker's Approach

USED BOOKS. A dry-erase board. That ignored supply closet at the end of the hall. A 99-cent notebook. A smartphone. The contents of the ordinary teacher's life are not being used to their fullest potential. Although state-level policy changes, expensive new programs, and district-wide initiatives can significantly improve our work as educators, we don't have to wait for these things to start solving problems that make an already difficult job even more challenging. Some of our biggest, most persistent obstacles can be overcome by using the things that are right under our noses, more creatively.

In this book, we have gathered 10 powerful ideas, or hacks, for solving education-related problems. Each hack shows you how to take the objects, systems, and people who are already available to you and repurpose, reorganize, or reimagine them to creatively address problems. Technology does come into play, but only sometimes: In four of the hacks, free technology tools are an integral part of the solution, but the other six require no technology at all. Anyone—regardless of his or her tech skills—will find something useful here.

YOU, A HACKER?

Who is the YOU we are speaking to in this book? Who is our intended audience? If we're offering solutions to problems in education, does that mean only administrators should read this book? Absolutely not. More than a collection of ideas, this book represents a philosophy: *We no longer live in a time when educators have to wait for the people in charge to solve problems.* Sure, some solutions still require months of meetings and need piles of paperwork to change hands before changes can be made, but the hacks in this book can be implemented by anyone. You don't have to be an administrator to get these rolling. In fact, the people in charge may not be convinced that an idea has merit until after an individual teacher has tried it.

If you are one of those teachers, surrounded by colleagues who may not be eager to run with new ideas, then find ways to try them yourself. If your administrator is not ready to move meetings to the cloud, as we suggest in Hack 1, see if you can move one meeting you have planned with a colleague. If no one at your school is interested in setting up a school-wide Book Nook (Hack 8), haul an extra bookshelf into your classroom and start your own there. All of the hacks in this book can be tweaked and developed into a whole-school program, but they can also be scaled down, so that individual educators can still try them.

> Embrace the concept of iteration, of continually reviewing and reworking a solution until it becomes the perfect fit for your particular needs.

THE IMPORTANCE OF BETA TESTING AND ITERATION

The ideas presented in this book are frameworks, not rigid prescriptions. They are designed to be built upon and improved, flexible enough for further development and adaptable to your individual situation. That's what hackers do—they take an idea and try different things with it, continually working on problems until a robust solution has been built.

When software engineers develop new applications, they usually go through what's known as a beta phase. When software is "in beta," it has all of its basic parts, but is being user tested to work out the kinks and find the bugs. The beta concept can be applied to any new program, tool, or system; for best results, it should be applied to your hack as well. Instead of waiting for the perfect time to implement it, or waiting until you've done extensive training and practice and have everything in place, why not just try it? Launch it in beta and see how it goes. When problems arise, remind yourself that this new initiative is in beta; problems can and should be seen as opportunities to learn and improve.

Once you've gotten through the beta phase, try it again: This is your second version of the hack, the next iteration, where some of the bugs have been fixed and the hack has been fine-tuned. Taking an iterative approach is so much better than what we often see with education initiatives: We try it once, decide it doesn't work, and abandon it. Instead, embrace the concept of iteration, of continually reviewing and reworking a solution until it becomes the perfect fit for your particular needs.

BOOST YOUR HACK WITH BRANDING

When working to implement a hack in your school, the idea is likely to be more successful if you spend a little time branding it. In the same way that Maroon 5 promotes an upcoming concert or Martha Stewart packages a new line of table linens, put some thought into how your hack might be packaged so it will grab people's attention more quickly and drum up more curiosity.

The teachers in the first Marigold Committee (Hack 6) branded themselves by wearing felt marigold pins to faculty meetings and other whole-faculty events. And though it would still work the same way without it, the Pineapple Chart (Hack 2) has been branded with a pineapple. Both of these hacks would serve the same purpose without their branding, but they might not have the sticky quality that all hacks need.

If you're excited about the hack you've chosen and want others to experience your enthusiasm, think about giving your hack a name, a launch date, and a proper promotion with well-designed posters or web pages, cleverly crafted video or P.A. announcements, and other packaging that will send the message that this idea is fresh, new, and exciting. The buzz you create will make stakeholders feel invested in the project and build community, which is so important to every school.

WHERE DID THESE HACKS COME FROM?

While a few of these solutions came from our own practice as teachers, others are just good ideas we've curated, solutions we've heard about that others are using, hacks that are so impressive that they have to be shared so you can try them.

As with all "new" ideas, most of these hacks build on concepts you may already be familiar with. In fact, someone you know might already be using one of these ideas, or some variation of it. That's fine. We don't claim ownership of these hacks—it's the ideas that matter, and they deserve to be shared and developed. If everyone who heard a new idea kept it quiet for fear of running into someone who was already trying it, ideas would spread far more slowly than they often do. Imagine if Mark Zuckerberg had decided that social media was not new (ever heard of MySpace?); Facebook might be nothing more than a magazine full of selfies. For every person who sniffs that an idea is "nothing new," there are ten more who have never heard of it. It's the variations, the iterations, that can make an old idea fresh again.

WHICH HACK WILL BE YOURS?

Our hope is that each of these hacks will excite and inspire you, make you feel empowered, and open your mind to what's possible in your school. Although we realize all 10 hacks are not likely to suit every person who reads this book, the truth is that if even one takes hold in your school and solves a problem that was once seen as unsolvable, the book will have earned its keep.

It's in here: One of these hacks will grab you, make you set this book aside, pick up your phone or open up an email to contact someone, another person with the same hacker mentality as yours, and say, "I think I found it."

Which one will it be? There's only one way to find out.

MEET ME IN THE CLOUD

Replace Meetings with a Backchannel and a Bin

Time is what we need most but what we use worst.
—WILLIAM PENN, ENGLISH ENTREPRENEUR

THE PROBLEM: LONG, TIME-CONSUMING MEETINGS

TIME. EVERY TEACHER wants more of it. The demands on teachers' time seem to grow each year, making it nearly impossible to do the things that are essential for effective teaching: strategic planning, giving thoughtful feedback on student work, learning new methods, collaborating with other teachers, reflecting on our practice, and taking care of our own health, families, and homes in order to be fully present at school.

If you're like most teachers, a lot of the "free" time that's supposed to be designated for these crucial tasks is robbed by meetings. Take a moment to consider anything you do in school that can be categorized as a meeting.

Here are a few examples:

- faculty/staff meeting
- department meeting
- grade level meeting
- committee meeting
- parent/teacher meeting

In a typical school, teachers will spend at least two hours per week in meetings. Now consider how much of that time you're thinking "We're wasting time here," or "I don't really need to hear this part." Every face-to-face meeting contains announcements for other people, discussions on topics that don't concern you, and waiting for that one person who goes on and on to finally take a breath. Add to this the minutes spent waiting for stragglers to show up at the beginning and the last-minute conversations you get sucked into when you should be heading out the door, and you've got yourself a maddening accumulation of wasted time.

Imagine how many hours would be reclaimed if you could still access the information you need, but eliminate these meetings.

THE HACK: MOVE MEETINGS TO THE CLOUD

By setting up a cloud-based bin for storing data and documents, and a backchannel for open discussion, you effectively replace all the components of a face-to-face meeting while also removing all the waste. "Eliminate" may be a bit misleading. Meetings aren't really being discarded; they're simply being moved to a different environment, one that doesn't require your physical presence.

Here's how it works: Suppose you are in charge of an upcoming meeting. Your first step is to write an agenda. Instead of creating it on a desktop computer, construct it in a folder in whatever cloud storage system you choose (Google Drive, Dropbox, etc.). We're calling this folder a *bin*. Invite anyone who might want to collaborate on the initial agenda to the bin, where they can add comments to it. As the "meeting" date approaches, add other items to the bin—whatever would normally be a handout in a face-to-face meeting. If you want participants to read an article or watch a video that lives somewhere else online, simply add links to your agenda. If there are questions that need to be discussed, indicate this in the agenda. When all the documents are ready, send a link to the bin to all meeting participants, giving them a date for completion.

> A backchannel is a discussion platform that allows for back-and-forth conversation between multiple parties.

Meanwhile, establish a *backchannel*, so all meeting participants can easily interact with one another. A backchannel is a discussion platform that allows for back-and-forth conversation between multiple parties (two examples are Voxer, a walkie-talkie-style voice platform, and TodaysMeet, which allows users to set up a temporary dialogue online). The discussions can take place in a whole-group chat, where all participants are included, and in smaller groups for more specific topics. Launch the "meeting" by delivering opening remarks and announcements in the whole-group chat, sort of like a brief keynote address.

Then, over the next few days, participants access the bin at whatever time is convenient for them, following the instructions in the agenda and completing whatever tasks are assigned to them by the completion date. For discussion items, participants will talk either in the whole- or small-group chats, depending on the topic.

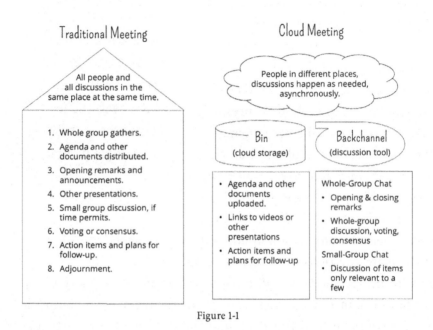

Figure 1-1

When the completion date arrives, close the "meeting" with some final remarks on the whole-group chat, letting everyone know what was decided and what documents are available in the bin for further reading or downloading. It might sound something like this: "Great meeting, everyone. The Special Ed department met and decided they will be doing week-long rotations of supervisory duty from now on; they have posted their new schedule in the bin. Also, the holiday potluck has been scheduled for December 18th. Please go to the form in the bin if you'd like to sign up to bring something."

WHAT **YOU** CAN DO TOMORROW

Eliminating your biggest meetings will take some time and adjustment for everyone, but you can start small by taking these steps right away:

- **Shift one agenda item.** Consider the next small-group meeting you have planned. Tell all participants that you are going to shift *one* major agenda item to the cloud.

- **Set up the system.** Choose one backchannel and one bin (see examples in the Hack section) and make sure all participants have set up accounts and can access both.

- **Try it.** Put two things in the bin: a page of instructions for what people need to discuss in the backchannel, and whatever pertinent documents they might need to look at to inform that discussion. All tasks must be completed by the time the face-to-face meeting is set to occur. Remember, you are only moving one item to the cloud this time.

- **Debrief.** At the face-to-face meeting (the one from which you pulled this single item), talk about how the process went and discuss what can be done better the next time around.

A BLUEPRINT FOR FULL IMPLEMENTATION

Step 1: Explain Meeting in the Cloud.

Inform staff members that you want to build more time into teachers' work days and take advantage of the power of cloud-based learning. Remember, this is a good thing, so if you encounter any resistance, be sure to emphasize the importance of saving time and giving people more control over their own schedules.

Step 2: Offer professional development for any cloud-based communication systems.

Since these will house information and engage teachers in conversation, it's critical to ensure that everyone understands how to use them. YouTube is filled with simple how-to videos on just about any tool you'll adopt. Share these links with teachers and find go-to people who can coach the use of the tools. In fact, while this may seem counterintuitive, you might want to launch the elimination of meetings at a meeting. It might be fun to brand this somehow; maybe call it "The last meeting you'll ever attend." Turn this face-to-face meeting into PD and teach your staff how to use your new cloud-based system.

Step 3: Create subgroups.

The problem with large faculty meetings is that most agenda items rarely apply to every staff member. So don't repeat this mistake in the cloud: The rebranded meeting should be a source of excitement, not a maelstrom of unnecessary message alerts that ultimately make people tune out. Set up one "All Staff" folder in the bin and one "All Staff" chat group on the backchannel; then, create separate subgroups and subfolders for departments, teams, or any combination of people you need. The possibilities are endless. Just as in an all-staff meeting, some agenda items will only be "assigned" to certain subgroups; everyone else can bypass them entirely.

Step 4: Start small.

Trying to shift whole meetings to the cloud right away, without practice or adjustment, is likely to fail. Instead, it may be better to start by piloting just a few items—things that might be time-consuming in a face-to-face meeting—and gradually work your way up to whole meetings. Expect some bumps in the road as people adjust to the change, but try not to backslide: Think persistent, patient, forward movement, and remind everyone that the reward for their efforts will be *time*.

Step 5: Moderate the backchannel, and keep your bins tidy.

Especially in the beginning, before a smooth workflow and clear protocols have been established, those in charge should carefully monitor activity in the backchannel to make sure participation is effective and appropriate. Some participants may take things in a direction others feel is too social, while others may consume more than their fair share of airtime. Rather than treat these as transgressions, engage participants in regular discussion about what effective and appropriate participation looks like.

Similarly, it's important to keep your bins well organized. Assign someone to be in charge of each bin: Have this person remove files that are not relevant to the task at hand, archive inactive documents, and label items in a way that makes them easy to identify. When a participant goes into a bin full of outdated, irrelevant, or poorly labeled files, they have a harder time finding what they need; this can lead to inconsistent participation.

Step 6: Establish deadlines and accountability.

Attendance and participation in cloud-based meetings will work much better if people know exactly what they have to do, and when tasks should be completed. When creating your meeting agenda, provide clear instructions for each item: If people need to contribute a vote or opinion on an item in the backchannel, give them a time limit for sharing their thoughts. If a subgroup needs to make a decision on an issue, set a deadline for that group to submit their decision. If participants simply need to read an announcement, no further action may be required, but be sure all participants understand that this is where announcements will be made from now on. To increase the likelihood that people read these, you might plant a few treats that reward those who read carefully. For example, make the third announcement something like this: *The first five people who e-mail me with the subject line "Parking" will get to use a premium parking spot next week.*

OVERCOMING PUSHBACK

Because meetings are such an integral part of school culture, the suggestion to drastically reduce them may cause some opposition. Here are some likely objections and our suggestions for responding to them:

Some people won't "attend." Sure, in a face-to-face meeting, you have physical proof that everyone is present, but how *present* are they, really? How many people are surreptitiously marking papers, texting, catching up on emails or scrolling through their Facebook news feed? When people are forced to sit through meetings that have little relevance to them, they usually find ways to make that time valuable, even if they have to sneak it.

By contrast, cloud-based meetings can generate evidence of participation from 100% of attendees in the form of submitted documents and commentary in the backchannel. The recommendations in the previous section for deadlines and accountability measures can go a long way toward making participation in cloud-based meetings *more*—not less—active.

We'll miss the opportunity to socialize and build rapport. What's so great about relocating meetings to the cloud is that it means face-to-face meetings can be planned only for team-building, high-intensity collaboration, and fun. Imagine how differently your staff would feel about a weekly 30-minute "after school snack" social where individual staff members are recognized for personal milestones or professional achievements, rather than a full hour of announcements and PowerPoints.

Some staff members are not tech-savvy. If professional development and training are done well and continued support is offered, this can be overcome. Acknowledge the anxiety that some may feel about trying something new; simply feeling that their concerns are heard can inspire people to step outside of their comfort zone. If you take our advice and start slowly, you'll get everyone used to operating in a different environment. And if some faculty don't have the hardware to participate—for example, smartphones or tablets if you choose an app that requires these—have these folks borrow devices from colleagues for 15 minutes at a time, or see if you can arrange to let them check out school devices during "meeting" times.

Sometimes we just have to meet. Consider a meeting you might be planning. Check your agenda carefully. Now, ask yourself, "Is there anything here that absolutely can't be shared in the cloud? Do you have hard copies that can't be uploaded to a Dropbox or Google Drive folder?" Why not reach out to staff via your cloud-based communication tool and invite them to drop by the office or your classroom and retrieve them before the end of the day? This puts time management back in the hands of staff members.

THE HACK IN ACTION

The workflow we used to write this book serves as a wonderful model of how people can fully collaborate without ever setting foot in the same room. Before we wrote a single word of *Hacking Education*, we discussed the book's concept at length on Voxer. While waiting for our kids to finish extracurricular activities, taking care of household tasks, or killing time while pumping gas, we engaged in a weeks-long, back-and-forth conversation to develop the ideas that would eventually become this book.

When we were ready to begin drafting the chapters, we opened up a shared folder on Google Drive and started with one big, sloppy "brainstorming" document, each of us adding our own ideas and commenting on the other's. Eventually, that document became a table of contents, and new docs were opened up for individual chapters.

We divided responsibility for the chapters, consulting with each other as needed. If Mark was finished drafting a chapter, he would send Jennifer a vox to let her know it was ready for her feedback, describing which areas he felt needed special attention. She could then jump into the document and add written comments in the margins, ready for Mark to consider when he was prepared to continue working. Similarly, if Jennifer was working on a different chapter and wanted to head in a direction that deviated from the original plan, she would send a Voxer message to share her thoughts with Mark, then head back into the chapter after a consensus had been reached.

Meanwhile, we also "met" about the book's design. Working with a designer—a third person we never met face-to-face—we created a secret Pinterest board and started pinning images each of us liked. The designer was able to look at these and come up with some mock-up designs for the book's cover. With a combination of Voxer exchanges and written comments on the designs pinned to the board, we made a final decision on how this book would look, without a single face-to-face meeting.

On most days, these discussions happened asynchronously—one person would leave a vox or a written comment at 7 a.m., the other would respond 15 minutes later, and the response to that would come an hour or two after that, each of us fitting the conversation in whenever it was most convenient for us. On other days, we'd find ourselves sitting at our desks at the same time—often by chance, occasionally by appointment—with the same document open on both of our screens and our phones in hand, voxing back and forth about a specific section of the book.

It was as if we were in the same room together, but in some ways even better: If one of us had to get up and run an errand, the conversation could still continue for a bit longer if needed—with Voxer on our phones, we could just carry the "meeting" with us. Although we had collaborated with others on cloud-based documents before, we were both continually amazed by how much faster and more effective our work became with the addition of Voxer.

By combining backchannel discussions with the easy accessibility of cloud storage, you can truly replicate the dynamic of face-to-face meetings. For busy teachers and administrators whose work depends on robust collaboration, but who hate setting aside hours and hours to do it, moving meetings to the cloud can be a real game changer.

PINEAPPLE CHARTS

Boost Teacher Collaboration with a Public Chart of "Open Door" Lessons

Alone we can do so little; together we can do so much.
— HELEN KELLER

THE PROBLEM: LITTLE TO NO PEER OBSERVATION

TEACHERS ARE CONSTANTLY searching for new ideas, solutions to problems with classroom management, organization, and instruction. "I need to figure out how to get my students to understand this concept," they say, or "I need to find someone who knows how to do _____." Time and money for professional development are both in short supply, but too often the most valuable resource—the teacher next door—is completely ignored.

The idea of observing other teachers is nothing new. It's the way we all first started learning how to teach, and you'd be hard-pressed to find a teacher who hadn't learned *something* from sitting in a colleague's classroom. Observing each other teach is one of the easiest and fastest ways to refresh our practice, learn new strategies, and build rapport with one another. And although many teachers say their door is always open, most of the time we never leave our own classrooms.

One reason for this is that everyone is busy—time is such a valuable commodity and no one has enough extra time to find out what another teacher is doing and plan a visit. The other reason is payoff: Even with the teacher whose door is always open, how do you know what she's doing on any given day? There's too much risk of showing up at the wrong time, interrupting something that really shouldn't be interrupted, or going all the way across the building, then settling in to observe a lesson that you quickly realize isn't all that relevant to you.

If only there were a way to see, at a glance, what other teachers are doing right now in your building. A way to know at a moment's notice whose door is open for observation and what's going on inside. A way to decide, if you have a few minutes to spare, where you might go to see some really interesting teaching.

THE HACK: POST A CALENDAR OF "OPEN HOUSE" LESSONS

The pineapple is a traditional symbol of welcome. When it's displayed on welcome mats and on door hangings, the intended message is "Come in! All are welcome here." A Pineapple Chart is a systematic way to put a "welcome mat" out for all classrooms, a central message board that lets other teachers know that you're doing something worth watching today, and if they'd like to come by, your door is open.

> What's even better is that this system is dynamic and customizable; it's the exact opposite of a one-size-fits all PD.

The chart would be something like a dry-erase board, sectioned off with tape or wet-erase marker into days of the week and class periods. The board would be kept near teacher mailboxes, the copier, or some other high-traffic area for staff. Every week, teachers would add their own classroom activities that others might like to see. These could be lessons in which the teacher is trying a new instructional strategy, when a new technology tool will be used, when students will be actively creating something, or even just when an interesting topic will be covered. This offers other teachers a menu of options for informal observations and allows them to visit places where they have a high interest.

🍍	Mon	Tue	Wed	Thu	Fri
1		Taylor: Reciprocal Learning			
2	Hughes: Socratic Circles			Silva: Video Editing in iMovie	Silva: Video Editing in iMovie
3		Vasquez: Ellis Island Simulation	Vasquez: Ellis Island Simulation		
4	Turner: Impressionism		Miller: Frog Dissection	Miller: Frog Dissection	
5				Wilson: Measuring heart rate	
6	Robertson: Poetry Slam	Patel: Kahoot quiz	Robertson: Discussion of Lord of the Flies		
7		Patel: Kahoot quiz			

Figure 2-1

When other teachers see something on the board, they know they have explicit permission to stop by that class during that period to informally observe. They can stay as long as they like—even just a few minutes—and when they're ready to go, they go. That's the end: No paperwork, no post-observation conference, just a visit to see what's going on in other classrooms.

This system offers endless possibilities for learning. Teachers might observe someone in their content area for specific strategies they can use themselves. They can also watch a class in a different subject or grade level to pick up ideas on classroom management, organization, or strategies that can be transferred across curricular lines. Some teachers might sit in on a class because the topic just interests them—how often have you heard people say they wish they could go back and take their high school history classes again? In some cases, a teacher who is trying something new or dealing with a difficult behavior issue might ask observers for feedback. And other times, observations might occur when a teacher just wants to see a friend teach—peer observation can be a true bonding experience.

What's even better is that this system is dynamic and customizable; it's the exact opposite of a one-size-fits all PD. Each week, teachers make their own decisions about what they need or are interested in. If they have a packed schedule for several weeks, they may not do any observing at all, but when time is available (or an especially interesting lesson motivates them to *make* time), they can take advantage of something that meets their own specific needs.

There's one more benefit to Pineapple Charts and peer observation: Having teachers join each other in the classroom sets a wonderful example of collaboration and lifelong learning for our students. When another teacher visits and students ask why, explaining the rationale sends the message that teachers are always looking for ways to learn and improve, and they're doing it together, just as they hope students will.

WHAT **YOU** CAN DO TOMORROW

A full-blown, self-running Pineapple Chart will take some time to grow, but you can try a quick pilot version this way:

- **Post your Pineapple Chart.** Grab a sheet of notebook paper, poster paper, or even a dry-erase board you have lying around. Hang it up in a location where most teachers are likely to see it.

- **Ask a key question.** Across the top, write "What's going on in your class today? What time will that be happening?"

- **Recruit one or two teachers.** Ask them to write down something interesting they are teaching that day—a topic, an activity, or a strategy—and what time of day they are doing it. If you are a teacher, you should be the first one to share!

- **Send the word.** Using an all-staff e-mail or an all-call on the P.A. system, announce to staff that this paper exists, that Ms. _____ is doing _____ in her room today and welcomes visitors, and encourage other staff members to add their activities to your makeshift Pineapple Chart.

A BLUEPRINT FOR FULL IMPLEMENTATION

Step 1: Set the stage.

Explain the overall process of the chart to the staff. This can be initiated by an administrator or a single teacher (with admin permission). Be clear that this is nothing like formal observations, where there can be job-related consequences. The point of the Pineapple Chart is to encourage everyone to share their ideas and practices with others.

Step 2: Create the chart.

Ideally, this would be a large whiteboard hung in a prominent location, with dry-erase markers readily available. (Think about those big surgery schedules you see on TV hospital shows.) Along the left-hand column, divide the chart by class periods or time-frames, however your school sets up its day. Across the top, divide the chart by the days of the week.

Step 3: Recruit early adopters.

For this to work, your school needs a team of enthusiastic participants to get things going. Privately recruit two groups: teachers who are not shy about having visitors in their classroom and are willing to add their names and activities to the chart when it's still a big blank space, and another group who will commit to making visits and talking them up with colleagues throughout the building. Have these teachers get the chart going, but be sure everyone understands that the chart is open to anyone.

Step 4: Encourage others to participate.

After the first wave has passed, it may be necessary to gently push others to join in. Although participation should be strictly optional, if you hear about a teacher who is trying something new in her classroom, suggest that she add the lesson to the chart. And if you know of a few teachers who never make observation visits, find one you believe would be a good fit for them and ask if they'd like to go with you.

Step 5: Make room for reviews.

Create time and space for teachers to share positive reviews of their visits. This can take many forms, like setting aside five minutes at the start of every faculty meeting to let people describe something great they saw that week, or adding a second board beside the Pineapple Chart where people can write or pin comments and reflections about specific visits.

Reflections might look something like this: "Go see the Cubist paintings in Heldic's room—amazing!" or, "Really enjoyed watching students play with Kahoot in Mr. Bowen's class today." Tech enthusiasts might reflect in a cloud-based location, like a shared Google Doc where people continually add their own comments about things they learned, or a "Database of Expertise," a spreadsheet where specific skills are listed (like flipping the classroom or cooperative learning) along with recommendations of people who are especially good at them.

Step 6: Incentivize it.

Over the long term, teachers could be given incentives for participation (as observers or hosts) in the form of professional development credit, being relieved of supervision duties ("10 visits = one day off bus duty!"), or other surprises, like the administrator brings you breakfast or a grab-bag of coupons from local businesses. These are marvelous ways to make professional development fun, and what teacher doesn't love fun PD?

OVERCOMING PUSHBACK

Making Pineapple Charts work well requires staff participation, and for some teachers, that means getting past these hurdles:

I'm too self-conscious to have people watch me teach. That's fine. Seriously. If some people never want to write their names on the board, don't pressure them. If this becomes something mandatory, people will resist. Those who are more shy about having visitors will still get a lot from going to watch other people teach. And if you emphasize and model positive feedback, and incentivize the program, eventually people will start to realize that only good things can come from the classroom visits.

I don't do anything interesting enough. Some people may get the impression that only the most innovative lessons are worth putting up on the board, and that they have nothing to offer. This is where your early adopters come in: Make sure that the first few people who put their lessons up include some things that might be considered ordinary. You never know what might attract someone. A basic lecture on Roman architecture might entice an art teacher who has a special interest in that topic. And your reputation for a beautifully organized classroom or creative discipline strategies might be the reason someone comes to your room—the topic might just give them an excuse to show up.

This is one more thing we have to do. No, it isn't. Remember, participating in Pineapple Chart visits is never mandatory. It's fun, simple, and optional. The draw to visit should come from the learning activities themselves, not pressure from administrators.

What if I visit someone's room and end up not liking it after a few minutes? Make it understood ahead of time that visits can be as short as five minutes or as long as a full class period. Be sure everyone is clear ahead of time that someone leaving after a short time doesn't mean your lesson isn't good; they might only have a few minutes, or they might not find it relevant.

Education unconferences like Edcamps have an understood "rule of two feet," where people are encouraged to get up and leave sessions whenever they decide the information is not relevant to them, and session leaders are strongly encouraged to leave their egos at the door and not take it personally! If your early adopters model a relaxed, truly open-door attitude, it will quickly become contagious.

I can't give up my planning time to observe another teacher. Indeed, everyone is short on time. That's just one more reason *not* to force teachers to visit. Since this is not a formal observation and you're not obligated to complete paperwork, it's perfectly fine to sit in the back of another teacher's room and grade papers or catch up on email; you can absorb a lot just by being in the room. Because this is not a formal observation, no one needs to give 100 percent attention to what's going on—you're there to pick up a few new ideas, get a feel for how someone else does things, see your students in a new light, and show an interest in what your peers are doing. If multitasking is the only way to make that happen, then multitask you must.

THE HACK IN ACTION

At Woburn Memorial High School in Woburn, Massachusetts, teachers began using the Pineapple Chart in the spring of 2015. "There was a ton of enthusiasm as soon as we shared the idea with the staff," says Abby Morton, the earth science teacher who introduced the chart. And not long after the chart was posted, teachers started visiting each other's classrooms.

Just as in the example above, Morton had to recruit a few of her fellow teachers to take the lead in signing their names to the chart, but soon other names appeared as well, and the visits began. "People always talked about wanting to see each other's lessons, but it's like so many other things in teaching—if you don't plan it, it doesn't happen."

Woburn's early experiences demonstrate the versatility and cross-curricular potential of the Pineapple Chart. One of the first visits was when an ESL teacher came to visit Morton's classroom to observe a science lesson. "I was struck by her open, comfortable teaching style, and in the way she encourages all to take part in the discussion," the visiting teacher reported. Despite the fact that the two work in different content areas, the visiting ESL teacher picked up some ideas that go beyond the curriculum.

Peer observation is one of the most powerful, affordable forms of professional development. By offering teachers an easy way to find the exact learning activities that interest them at a time that fits their schedule, Pineapple Charts make peer observation available to everyone, all the time.

HACK 3

TEACHER QUIET ZONES

Escape the Chaos and Maximize Planning Time

*The monotony and solitude of a quiet life
stimulates the creative mind.*
—ALBERT EINSTEIN

THE PROBLEM: NO SANCTUARY

THE FRENETIC PACE of the typical school day brings a cornucopia of noise and distraction. Sure, this is the nature of school and some chaos should be embraced, but at some point during a teacher's day, quiet is needed for planning, grading, and simply getting centered. In fact, most teachers have a portion of each day designated as prep time. But just as meetings steal hours away from other important tasks, noise and disruption often interfere with teachers' time to plan, adding a certain degree of angst to what is already a stressful job.

Over the course of a five-day work week, simple disruptions tear chunks out of planning time: Students waltz into your classroom uninvited, just to say hello. Colleagues loiter around your desk, venting about what went wrong with a lesson. An announcement blares,

43

destroying the solitude that is necessary for deep thought and effective planning. These kinds of interruptions have become so commonplace, we have come to expect very little from our planning periods. Some teachers have given up trying to get anything done at school, opting instead to take work home.

Maybe it doesn't have to be this way. When teacher time is sacrosanct, building-wide efficiency increases exponentially. Is there any way to guarantee teachers the uninterrupted time they need to do their jobs at peak effectiveness?

THE HACK: CREATE TEACHER QUIET ZONES

In any school building, a room or section can be designated as a Teacher Quiet Zone, a place where it is understood that teachers are not to be disturbed.

Think of the Teacher Quiet Zone (TQZ) like you would a library or a monastery, where silence and solitude typically dominate. This is an area where teachers literally escape the chaos of school. Unlike the faculty lounge, the mailroom, or the traditional teacher workroom, the quiet zone is designed with one key concept in mind: absolute silence. It's where teachers go to do the kind of focused, uninterrupted work they may not be able to do in their classrooms, to meditate or read, or perhaps just slow down and enjoy a few peaceful moments. It is your haven for all things calm and quiet.

The Teacher Quiet Zone may be the hackiest of hacks because of its sheer simplicity. All you need is a small space and a general consensus.

WHAT YOU CAN DO TOMORROW

Establishing a permanent TQZ will take some creativity and will require adjustment in the mindset of some staff members, but you can get a taste for the benefits of this hack by following these steps:

- **Locate your getaway.** Find a space in your building that is typically vacant for some chunk of the school day: a rarely-used storage room, a conference room, a large closet, or a classroom that is unused during a predictable time. Unless you have no other options, avoid using your own classroom for this purpose.

- **Invite friends.** Find a few other staff members who would be interested in doing a test run of a TQZ with you. Using e-mail or your favorite faculty communication tool, announce that for one day only, Conference Room B (or whatever your designated area is) will be blocked off as a Teacher Quiet Zone, and that any teacher found there should be left undisturbed. Invite other staff members to use the room, but be clear that any talking should be taken outside the TQZ. Sell the idea as a great option for teachers who are looking for a refuge.

- **Try it.** Use your temporary TQZ and remember the idea of iteration: If some aspects of the TQZ don't work quite right, see these as opportunities for improvement, rather than reasons to abandon the project.

A BLUEPRINT FOR FULL IMPLEMENTATION

Step 1: Build a team of early adopters.

Talk to a few colleagues about the value of a TQZ. Most people may have been longing for something like this for quite a while and will love the idea. The more people you have on board, the more likely it is that an administrator won't dismiss the idea as unnecessary.

Step 2: Enlist an administrator.

Consider going to an assistant principal with this idea before approaching the senior administrator. You can hand your proposal to the AP, who can easily pass it to the principal when she's not too busy to entertain this kind of innovation, which may be too easy to push to the bottom of a priority list if presented at the wrong time. Be sure to emphasize that silence, meditation, and reflection are crucial to the success of teachers, who can be easily overwhelmed by the daily stress that the job brings.

Step 3: Set rules for your TQZ.

Even before anointing a space as your permanent Teacher Quiet Zone, it's important to create some rules. Make TQZ rules specific and place them on a large, bright, colorful poster board for all who enter to see. Here are some suggested rules, but you can add others as you see fit:

- The Teacher Quiet Zone (TQZ) is for teachers and other school personnel who desire silence.

- Refrain from talking, whispering, humming, or anything else that could be interpreted as noise. If your work is inherently noisy, please do it in another location.

- Silence your mobile device.

- Refrain from socializing in the TQZ. If you need to talk, please take the conversation outside the room.

- Students should remain outside of the TQZ.

Step 4: Find a space.

Once you've all decided on a few potential spaces for your new Teacher Quiet Zone, walk through each area and consider all elements that make the room a good fit. An effective TQZ requires only two key items:

- Comfortable seating for up to eight people (more if you have a large building with many people on planning periods at the same time)

- One or more spacious tables that can serve as work areas

Take a minimalist approach. Your TQZ doesn't need computers, printers, or copy machines. Remember, while the quiet zone may be used for work, it is for silent work. Desktop computers, printers and copiers are noisy. If technology is needed, stick to tablets or laptops. Printing and copying can be done elsewhere. If a single space isn't available, or if your school is so large that traveling to a single space would be too time-consuming for some faculty members, consider setting up several zones throughout the building. And if no spaces are available as permanent zones, set up a schedule of "rotating zones," where a sign can be hung outside of various rooms at different times, designating them as TQZs for that class period.

Step 5: Commit to the rules.

Have you ever been shushed in a library or church? For most people, this is an unpleasant experience. Still, one can hardly object when the rules are clear. Remind all staff members frequently, when necessary, that the TQZ is built for peace and quiet.

OVERCOMING PUSHBACK

The only thing that can interfere with the creation of a teacher quiet zone is lack of space, and even this can be overcome in virtually every school. Here are other issues that may arise:

> Teacher burnout and attrition are serious issues. Adding a little peace makes your crazy, super difficult job a little easier.

A TQZ is a waste of space; teachers can just work in their classrooms. Classrooms are rife with traffic and disruption. Can you remember a time you worked during a school day for 30 completely quiet minutes? Also, taking time out of the busy day for reflection and or meditation is an important part of maintaining a stress-free environment for all. Unlike classrooms and faculty lounges, the TQZ is designed to reduce teacher stress.

Sometimes people need to talk. Not in the quiet zone. If you must converse with someone in the room, quietly invite her to step outside of the TQZ. It's critical to be respectful to others and to the room. Treat it like a sanctuary.

What about taking important phone calls? Silencing mobile devices must be a strictly enforced rule. Rings should be quiet vibrations, and callees should exit the TQZ before answering.

I need tools to work and some are noisy by design. No problem. Work in your class or in a workroom that is not designated as the TQZ. Working in the quiet zone is voluntary. On your planning time, you can go anywhere you wish.

Sometimes secretaries or administrators will need to contact people in the TQZ. Send a student messenger, with strict instructions to knock and maintain quiet. Placing a phone or PA receiver in the room should be avoided.

What teacher has time for quiet reflection or meditation? The ones who value their health and sanity do. Teacher burnout and attrition are serious issues. Adding a little peace makes your crazy, super difficult job a little easier. Who knows? The TQZ might even extend your career.

THE HACK IN ACTION

Charles F. Brush High School in Lyndhurst, Ohio has an area that functions as a Teacher Quiet Zone. It isn't referred to precisely as this, but the design and rules are the same. This small area is tucked unobtrusively above the school's library; in fact, not many students know the room exists, making it a perfect location for a quiet zone for teachers. Some go there to read or work in silence. Others catch that all-important power nap. Talking is frowned upon, according to teachers who frequent the room. The key to its success, according to teachers and the librarians, who act as the room's guardians, is its restorative power. Teachers escape the chaos of classrooms, offices, and hallways, and enjoy what might amount to no more than 20 minutes of solitude. Then they return to work, feeling rejuvenated.

Sometimes the very thing you need to boost productivity and morale is *nothing*: Pure, private, undisturbed silence. Unlike experienced professionals in so many other industries, teachers don't have the luxury of an office with a door, a place to concentrate, reduce stress, and get things done. Since few schools will ever be able to foot the bill for a separate wing of private teacher offices, a Teacher Quiet Zone can go a long way toward meeting those same needs.

TRACK RECORDS

Make Classroom Management Enduring and Real with a Simple Notebook

The content of your character is your choice.
Day by day, what you choose, what you think
and what you do is who you become.
—HERACLITUS, GREEK PHILOSOPHER

THE PROBLEM: MANAGING MINOR MISBEHAVIORS

CLASSROOM MANAGEMENT IS one of the most challenging aspects of teaching. If a teacher can't get students to stay on task, treat each other civilly, follow basic instructions, and behave in a way that permits others to learn, there's little else they can do. Forget about innovative teaching practices; if students are climbing the walls and throwing shoes at each other, all you can focus on is getting them to stop throwing those shoes.

Okay, so maybe they're not throwing shoes. Maybe they're just tardy. Or they forget to bring supplies. Their homework is incomplete, late, or missing. They're whispering. Texting. Not following through. It's these little things that create problems for you as a teacher. What's worse, they will ultimately cause problems for the students. If students regularly make unproductive, disruptive, or careless choices, they are likely to struggle for the rest of their academic and professional careers, and they may never really understand why.

So what do you do about it? Many teachers use token or reward systems, or another kind of carrot, in an attempt to extrinsically motivate students to make good choices. Others are big proponents of the long lecture. Some teachers assign detention, take away privileges, and send kids to the office. Others just yell.

Regardless of the approach you take, one persistent question remains: Are we *permanently* changing behavior, or are students simply responding to punishments and rewards? Is there any way to teach students how to make good choices—both academic and non-academic— in a way that helps them internalize those habits? And can it be done without consuming tons of class time?

THE HACK: REPLACE PUNISHMENT AND REWARD WITH A TRACK RECORD

Instead of setting up a system of consequences for poor choices and rewards for good ones, let a student's track record become the motivator: Using a basic notebook, allowing one page for each student, simply document any student behaviors that are noteworthy. If a student comes to class five minutes late, record that on his page along with the date. If a student does not turn in her homework, write that on her page.

Keep track of good choices too: If a student holds a door open for his peers to walk through, make a note of this. If someone else disagrees with a classmate during a discussion in a way that is respectful and productive, record it. The "Track Record" notebook is not just for documenting poor choices. It's exactly what its name says: a track record—an accumulation of behaviors that constitute a person's general reputation.

Jane Doe		
Date	+	−
9/14	Offered a pencil to another student.	
9/30	Volunteered to give first speech.	
10/7		Tardy 2 min.
10/8		Tardy 3 min.
10/13	Stayed focused during silent reading.	Tardy 2 min.
10/14		Tardy 2 min.

Figure 4-1

After an observation is recorded, you can share your documentation with that student privately. This could involve pulling her aside for a moment, giving her a peek at her page, and saying, "Thank you for staying focused during silent reading today. I added that to your track record." Or, "Take a look at this. You've been tardy four times in the past week. What has changed? What's going on?" If an incident doesn't warrant an immediate conversation, you could set up a regular time (weekly, monthly, or once per marking period) to let students see their pages and discuss them with you.

This system is more reflective of what adults often refer to as the "real world," where making bad choices doesn't always result in immediately observable punishment. Adults who regularly interrupt others in conversation don't get put in detention for talking out of turn. Their consequences are more subtle: When it comes time to invite people for an intimate dinner, the interrupter's invitation may get lost in the mail. An employee who always arrives within a millisecond of her scheduled start time may not face disciplinary action, but she may be passed over when her boss is looking for someone to promote. By contrast, a driver with a spotless record who is pulled over for speeding is more likely to be let off with a warning than the person who has a glovebox full of parking violations. In all aspects of life, your track record—whether in writing or just stored in people's memories—speaks to your character. The sooner students start to see the big picture on this, the better off they'll be.

Using a Track Record to simply document student activity as it happens is a surprisingly effective way to encourage students to make better choices. Despite the fact that in most cases, the students receive no other consequence besides having their conduct recorded, many are bothered enough by having something negative written about them that they will naturally try to avoid it in the future. And the cumulative effect of multiple incidents being recorded together can be powerful: It's one thing to complain that a student is talking too much, but it's another matter entirely to tally the number of times you have to redirect that student back to her work and show her a grand total at the end of a class period. Or better yet, tell her you're going to be taking the tallies, and watch how drastically those incidents are reduced.

The Track Record has other benefits: For one, it provides necessary evidence of ongoing problematic behavior in cases where a student needs to be referred for disciplinary action. Administrators like to know that you have done everything you could to solve smaller problems in your own classroom before sending students to the office. By documenting behavior in a Track Record, you have proof that the problem has been ongoing.

What's more, recording *positive* behaviors can make well-behaved (and often ignored) students finally feel noticed, and it reinforces good choices in students who struggle with behavior. Adopting this practice will help you develop a more positive attitude toward a class that might, at first glance, appear to be out of control.

⚙ WHAT **YOU** CAN DO TOMORROW ⚙

Clearly, the value of a Track Record is its accumulation of observations over time, but you can start enjoying some of its benefits right away:

- **Grab a notebook.** As soon as you've gotten students started on a task that does not require your sustained involvement, pick up a notebook and open it to a fresh page. Draw a line right down the center. On the left side, begin recording observations of the positive behaviors you observe. On the right, record less desirable behaviors. For this first time, you can just keep the whole class on one chart. Tell students you're just going to keep track of what happens today, because you want to make sure you're noticing the good choices people are making as well as the problems.

- **Write what you see.** As you go about your normal routine, stop occasionally to jot down observations. If nothing noteworthy is happening, just write "Focused" and record the names of a few students who are really staying on task.

- **Share your notes.** If students ask what you are writing, feel free to share your notes with the individuals you are writing about, but if this detracts from class work too much, tell students you will discuss your notes with them at another time.

- **Reflect.** At the end of the day, look for patterns: Did you record more negative than positive behaviors? Did certain names appear more than once? This document can be used to set goals (such as "notice more positive behaviors") and to plan brief conversations with key students the following day.

A BLUEPRINT FOR FULL IMPLEMENTATION

Step 1: Set up your Track Record.

Create a system that will work best for you: Some teachers may prefer a full 3-ring binder, divided by class period if you are teaching the upper grades, where all students have their own page (like the one pictured in Figure 4.1). This system is nice for its symbolism: If students are accumulating a lot of negative incidents, you could have a talk with them about the patterns they have gotten into and then "wipe the slate clean" with a fresh, empty sheet, filing away the old one in a separate location. For other teachers, a table or chart may work better, where each student has his or her own row. One column in the chart would be reserved for positive behaviors (indicated by the plus symbol), and the other for poor choices (the minus symbol).

If plusses and minuses or the terms "positive" and "negative" don't feel right to you, use whatever terminology or scale you like. You might choose to simply record observations without categorizing them as helpful or not. Just keep in mind that once you have recorded more than a few items, it will be more difficult to determine which choices were healthy, productive ones and which choices were not; having some kind of visual sorting system helps both you and the student recognize patterns right away.

Your Track Record can be kept on paper or in digital form, such as a Microsoft Word table, an Excel chart, or on a note-taking platform like Evernote—whatever works best for you.

Step 2: Choose your shortcut.

Whether you keep all your permanent notes in a binder or record them in an online document, quickly writing down events as they happen may require a more lightweight vehicle. This can be accomplished with a small notepad, a stack of post-it notes, a sheet of paper on a clipboard, or even your smartphone, where you can make short-hand notes to yourself, then transfer them to the Track Record later.

Step 3: Explain the system to students.

Doing this will make keeping the Track Record far more impactful than if students don't know about it. Start by explaining how in many situations in life, we don't receive small punishments or rewards for our behavior. Instead, we just develop a reputation, a track record that follows us wherever we go and influences how people judge us. You might even share the fable of the Boy Who Cried Wolf, in which a boy who played the same trick too often was not believed when he finally told the truth—his track record spoke for him.

Show students your record-keeping system—the chart or set of pages that have each of their names on them. Point out how the record is currently a blank slate —a "fresh start" that can be filled with positive or negative choices. Talk about the idea of a person's character being the sum total of his or her choices, and how everyone makes mistakes, but a *pattern* of poor choices suggests bigger problems.

Step 4: Record behaviors in neutral, objective terms.

Because the purpose of this record is to illustrate how repeated behaviors cumulatively form a person's general character, try not to add judgmental language when recording them. For example, instead of writing *Disruptive in class today*, which sounds like an opinion, write exactly what the student did: *Drummed fingers on desk 8 different times in one hour*. Similarly, for positive behaviors, instead of writing *Helpful in group work*, write *Spent 20 minutes teaching Prezi to another student*. Specific feedback, whether positive or negative, is far more instructive than general feedback.

Step 5: Be chill when documenting.

Calling a lot of attention to the act of recording a student's behavior—positive or negative—can backfire. An embarrassed student may actually start behaving worse in order to save face, resulting in a game where the student does something, you write it down, then they do something else, wait for you to write it down, and so on. Don't turn the Track Record into a sideshow. The point is to record observations without disrupting the flow of class, so make notes to yourself, then discuss them with the student later.

Step 6: Invite students to view their Track Records.

You might do this in regularly scheduled, brief conferences, or only on an as-needed basis. Use the Track Record as a tool for managing habits. For example, with a student who has recently developed a pattern of tardiness, show her the documentation, talk about the root cause of the lateness, and brainstorm some solutions. Then, to switch things up and change your focus to the positive, tell her you're going to track how many times she arrives *on time* for the next few weeks.

Step 7: Allow for "fresh starts."

If a student has accumulated a lot of negative documentation and wants a fresh start, let her have it. Replace crowded, blemished records with clean, blank ones and file the old ones away somewhere out of sight. This small gesture can be hugely symbolic to a student who is still figuring out who she is.

OVERCOMING PUSHBACK

I'm doing so many things already; I don't have time to add one more record-keeping system! If this system is put into place with good intentions, it is likely to *reduce* behavior problems, which will ultimately give you more time for instruction and other classroom activities. Still, you can create shortcuts that will reduce the amount of time you spend recording.

One way to do this is to create codes for frequent behaviors. For example, if a student is five minutes late, you could simply record the date and the code 5T for "five minutes tardy." Another way to save time is to use small post-it notes for your initial recording, then just stick them on the student's page at the end of the day, allowing you to skip the step of rewriting them. You might even have students record their actions on the post-it notes themselves, then sign them, building in another level of accountability.

What if kids see each other's pages? Privacy is an issue with all student records and documents, so treat your Track Record the same way you'd treat the rest of your private documents. If you are using a chart system rather than individual pages and want to show a student his or her record, simply zoom in the view on your computer screen so that only that student's row is visible. If this is too difficult, consider resizing the chart cells to make this process easier.

This sounds too negative and nit-picky; I'm not interested in keeping track of every little mistake my students make. Fair enough. If you already have a classroom management system that effectively deals with negative behavior, then you don't need this. Also, bear this in mind: You can record anything you want in this record. If you decide you only want to keep track of positive, constructive choices, you can do that. If you only want to record the most serious incidents rather than track many things every day, you can do that. What makes the Track Record different from other classroom management systems is that it is flexible.

What about really unacceptable behavior? I'm not going to walk away from a fistfight to write in a notebook! When faced with extreme or urgent misbehavior, handle it according to your school's discipline guidelines. Call the office, or write a referral, whatever is required for serious incidents. The Track Record is meant to manage smaller infractions.

THE HACK IN ACTION

Jennifer Gonzalez: I used this system when I taught college freshmen and sophomores. Part of my role teaching introductory education courses was to recommend students for entry into the education major. For each student, I had to complete a form evaluating them on academic skills, ethical behavior, punctuality, and other qualities that were viewed as important contributors to success in teaching.

At the end of each semester, when it came time to complete these forms, I sometimes struggled. Over the term, I had formed a general opinion about each student's habits and behaviors based on my experiences with them, but I hadn't always kept track of those things. When making decisions that could impact their careers, I wanted something more substantial to back up my ratings.

In my third year I created a record-keeping system like the one described in this hack. Using a simple chart created in Microsoft Word similar to the one pictured in Figure 4-1, I recorded late arrivals, early departures (which turned out to be quite frequent for some students), late or incomplete assignments, excessive socializing at inappropriate times, and occasions when students demonstrated a lack of attention to written instructions or e-mail communication. I also recorded times when students showed great enthusiasm for a class activity, took initiative by contacting me in advance if they were going to miss class, offered an especially relevant comment in a discussion, or requested additional clarification on an assignment. Each of these behaviors contributed to success in school and in life but are not always quantified in a student's grades.

When it came time to complete recommendation forms, I found these records to be incredibly useful in helping me make decisions about how to rate students. Later, when some of these same students came back to me requesting letters of recommendation for jobs, I was able to return to my chart and find specific examples of times when these students showed initiative or demonstrated the kinds of characteristics an employer would value.

The chart served another purpose as well: Because I told students about my system ahead of time, I found them to be more diligent about communicating with me than they had been in previous semesters. One student always seemed to have some kind of special event or activity causing her to miss class or to leave early, and I was able to pull up my record and show her that she had repeated similar requests multiple times over the semester. Seeing these incidents recorded one after another had an impact on her, and when I expressed concern that she didn't seem committed to the course, there was evidence to support this opinion. Had I not set up a Track Record, my observations could easily come across as an unfair bias against her.

Sometimes the best solution to a complex problem is the simplest. If setting up a system of consequences and rewards, tokens and demerits isn't a good fit for you, try the straightforward act of recording noteworthy incidents and showing your students that, ultimately, who we are really is the sum of the choices we make.

STUDENT TECH GURUS

Fix Small-Scale Tech Problems with a Team of Students

Don't limit a child to your own learning,
for he was born in another time.
—RABINDRANATH TAGORE, BENGALI WRITER, PHILOSOPHER, ARTIST, AND COMPOSER

THE PROBLEM: NOT ENOUGH TECH SUPPORT

TECHNOLOGY USE IN schools is growing at an exponential rate. Every year brings more opportunities for integrating technology into our teaching, and along with them come higher expectations for teachers. To meet those expectations, schools need two things: *training*, to learn how to operate the technology at the optimum level, and *support*, to address problems with hardware, software, and connectivity when issues arise.

Ideally, every school would employ a small staff of dedicated IT professionals who could provide training and solve problems when they occur. They could report to classrooms within minutes of a problem happening and quickly get things up and running again so that teaching and learning could continue.

Unfortunately, this is not the case in most schools. In some cases a school has only one person in charge of all the technology in the building; other districts require a single specialist to split their time between several schools. And many schools only have a default "tech person," someone whose original role was something else (librarian, career ed teacher) but who now has the added responsibility of managing building technology.

> Apart from troubleshooting, a team of student tech gurus can also work proactively, training students and staff in basic skills, so the whole school learns together.

This support shortage causes a whole host of problems, including lessons that have to be abandoned due to malfunctioning technology, hours of instructional time wasted while teachers try to solve problems on their own, or worse, the engaging hands-on activities that are *never planned in the first place*, because the risk of things not working is one many teachers aren't willing to take.

If teachers just had more knowledgeable people on call to fix problems when they crop up, they could take advantage of everything technology has to offer.

THE HACK: EMPLOY STUDENT TECH GURUS

Just like the kid who used to help with the classroom movie projector way back in the day, students can be trained to provide tech support to their classmates and teachers. Because many students are already comfortable with technology—often more so than their teachers—they can learn new tech skills quickly. This added support in every building means more lower-level problems get solved at a greater speed.

Although many teachers probably already enlist student help with classroom technology, it's likely that they use a "catch-as-catch-can" system: The teacher is having trouble getting a tool to cooperate, so a student jumps up, clicks a few things, and solves the problem. Imagine how much more effective this process could be if it was formalized, if a student tech support *team* was hand-picked, trained, and made available whenever it was needed. Apart from troubleshooting, a team of student tech gurus can also work proactively, training students and staff in basic skills, so the whole school learns together.

WHAT **YOU** CAN DO TOMORROW

Building a well-oiled student tech machine takes time, training, and planning, but you can start a loose pilot program right away:

- **Find the gurus.** Gather a small group of students whose tech skills you're already aware of. Their skills can be varied—remember, you're just trying out the concept. Make a list of the tools they know and can help with; for example, Prezi, Google Drive, Microsoft Word.

- **Inform your colleagues.** With the permission of your administrator, give this list to the whole staff or to a select group of teachers. Encourage them to reach out to these students for help with technology before contacting the school or district tech specialist.

- **Try on-the-spot "training."** If you have a few minutes to spare during class, ask for student volunteers to do 3- to 5-minute "show and tells" on a favorite website or app. This informal exercise has a big payoff: It will give students practice in presenting with technology, get other students used to learning tech from their peers, and help you identify skilled technologists who may also possess the necessary communication skills to explain "techy" concepts to "non-techy" people.

A BLUEPRINT FOR FULL IMPLEMENTATION

Step 1: Identify the team.

If you already have some kind of club or other group that focuses on technology, finding students to serve on a support team should be easy. Students on the team don't need to already know the exact tools or platforms required by the school, but they should demonstrate general aptitude with technology, the ability to pick up new skills, and good communication skills, since they will have to teach others. They also need to have strong academic and conduct records, because fulfilling their duties will mean missing some class time, and when giving assistance in other classrooms, they must be on their best behavior.

Step 2: Identify the school's needs.

Survey teachers and students to learn what problems they have most often, what new skills they most want to learn, and what their general needs are with respect to technology. Then choose two or three areas for your team to focus on first. The list of needs is likely to be long and varied, so look for patterns and frequent requests when deciding what your priorities will be. When creating your list of priorities, frame items as measurable goals. Here are some examples:

- Users will be able to log into Google Drive, create new items, share them with others, and upload, download, and move files.

- Users will be able to create new groups in Edmodo, send out announcements to groups, upload documents, and link to those documents in group announcements.

- Users will be able to set up a quiz on Kahoot, operate it in class, and save their results.

Along with your list of goals, brainstorm a set of possible frequently asked questions or problems that are likely to come up again and again.

Step 3: Train the team.

Once you have set clear, high-priority goals, train every member of your team until they have met each goal and can perform those tasks in their sleep. Be sure everyone can answer the list of frequently asked questions correctly. Finally, establish clear standards for conduct during help calls and role-play possible situations to give student helpers practice in giving assistance respectfully.

Step 4: Create the support team infrastructure.

Before telling anyone about the support team's services, set up the request infrastructure and a team workflow, so that when services are requested, those who need them get a timely response. Here's what should be included in your plan:

- A system for teachers and students to *submit their requests*. In 1987, this would be done with slips of paper and a shoebox. In 2004, requests may have been sent to the faculty sponsor's email address. Now, thankfully, we have other options: One way to do this is to set up a Google Form, then embed it somewhere on the school's website so that anyone who needs help can access it from anywhere. When teachers and students submit their requests through a Google Form, the information would automatically be sent to a spreadsheet. The tech support team could then check that spreadsheet and respond to requests as they come up.

- Devise a system for *assigning* help requests to student helpers. You might set up a schedule for students to be on call, or maybe the faculty sponsor will oversee the assignments, choosing helpers on a case-by-case basis.

- Set up a place to *document your work*. Keeping a running record of requests and how they were fulfilled allows you to track patterns, identify possible topics for training, and demonstrate your program's usefulness in the event that your district considers offering funds for expansion.

Step 5: Market your services.

People won't use student tech helpers if they don't know about them, so launch and maintain a marketing campaign to educate teachers and students about what services are provided and how they can access them. A good place to start is to create a tech team homepage somewhere on the school's website. Be sure to include a specific list of the skills your team is trained in, along with any specialty areas for individual team members. Is one of your support specialists especially good with PowerPoint? Advertise this!

You could also launch a more traditional ad campaign, with posters or announcements in the school newsletter. Consider how you might enlist *other* students in the marketing—artists and writers who may not excel at technology but can provide your team with compelling posters, scripts for short commercials, or other types of advertising. Because it will take time for people to become accustomed to the new system, be prepared to periodically re-educate the staff and students.

Step 6: Plan and deliver training.

Providing tech support to a school isn't just about reacting to problems as they come up; the support team can also train staff and students in the proper use of tools. These trainings can be conducted in large or small groups, delivered as part of faculty meetings, or given to individual classrooms. Trainings can also be recorded on video or offered as screencasts, which can be stored on the tech team's homepage.

OVERCOMING PUSHBACK

Our students are too young. Although student help desks are growing in popularity at the high school level, the trend has not trickled down to many middle and elementary schools, possibly because the staff believes it can't be done with younger students. At the elementary level, fifth and sixth graders are certainly mature enough to not only learn how to solve basic tech problems, but also to conduct trainings (you'll see this later in the Hack in Action part of this chapter).

Just imagine what a student would be capable of doing at the high school level if she already had experience serving in a tech support role in fifth grade! Younger students may not be able to provide support with as many tools as a high school team could, but they can still lighten the load on a school or district's need for support by solving the smaller problems. And if behavior is a concern, remember our recommendations to choose students with a history of good conduct and to clearly establish guidelines for behavior while serving in the tech support role.

What about security? Does doing this put our school's computers at greater risk? Keep in mind that this is a select group of students we're talking about, students who have already been vetted for their tech skills, academic records, and behavior, so they are less likely to make the kinds of mistakes that would threaten security–certainly no more likely than some of the less tech-savvy adults in the building! Still, they are kids, so if security is a concern, build safe practices into their training. You may feel that it's risky for the tech team to have access to confidential teacher documents (like student grades) when working on classroom computers. Be sure to train the teachers to close confidential files or log out of high-security portals when students will be accessing their computers.

If they're running around helping everyone, won't these tech kids miss too much class? By only recruiting students with strong academic records, you significantly reduce the chances that occasional absences will hurt grades. Just like any other extracurricular activity or sport, the faculty sponsor can create participation guidelines stating that students who do not maintain a certain grade average will be excused from the team until their grades come back up.

Also, if one particular subject area is off-limits for absences, or a certain teacher does not wish to release students for tech support, just build those considerations into your scheduling, making sure those students are not pulled at those times. One more thing to keep in mind: Even if students are missing some class time, they are still growing in their communication and technology skills, which will both be useful in their future academic and professional lives.

We don't have anyone in the building to train and supervise a student tech support team. This is a legitimate concern; one that will require a true hacker's mentality to address. Here are some possible solutions to this issue:

- If one person isn't willing or able to step up and facilitate this whole project, perhaps it could be managed by a small team of teachers, who could divvy up or rotate responsibilities.

- A tech-savvy teacher from some other school in your district could be given a few professional days to visit your school and train the team. Or on a larger scale, this person could train student teams for every school in the district, "meet" with them in the cloud (see Hack 1) to address day-to-day issues, then meet face-to-face with them periodically for training and troubleshooting.

- If it isn't possible to implement a full-fledged program with online request forms and formal trainings, every grade level (or team, in a middle school setting) might start by compiling a list of students who have specific tech skills and allow these students to be called on when smaller problems arise.

- The next time you have a faculty training about a particular type of technology, invite a small team of students to participate as well, so they can provide additional support as the staff works to implement the tool.

THE HACK IN ACTION

Students and teachers at Richardsville Elementary School in Bowling Green, Kentucky, enjoy the support of the Bobcat Help Desk, staffed by four tech-savvy sixth graders. Barry Sanders, library media specialist and sponsor of the school's Student Technology Leadership Program, established the Help Desk in 2014 as a way to satisfy the increasing requests for help from the faculty.

When the team formed, its first task was to survey the faculty in an effort to learn more about technology pain points. What they discovered was that most teachers wanted help learning to navigate Google Drive and work with their new Chromebooks. So the team developed a workshop to teach these skills, presenting it first as a whole-staff professional development session, then as a workshop given to individual classrooms in grades 3 through 6. To further extend their reach, the team has created video tutorials covering some of the same skills taught in their trainings.

Apart from the trainings, the team also responds to requests for assistance. The Bobcat Help Desk uses a workflow much like the one described in the blueprint above. Every school day, team members report to the library to check for any open "tickets"—help requests that have been submitted through the Google Form embedded on the school's website—which are then automatically dropped into a Google spreadsheet. From there, Sanders or the students decide who will respond to which request.

Nolan, Maddie, Tristan, and Natalie serve as the 6th Grade
Student Help Desk at Richardsville Elementary

So is the system working? Since the team was established, Sanders has seen the school's overall need for technology-related assistance drop dramatically: He estimates that their help requests to the district technology coordinators have dropped about 75 percent this school year. "If a problem is sent to the district, it's already been pre-screened by the students and me," Sanders says, "so it's definitely a more serious issue." This is a great way to speed up the workflow for everyone: Giving the smaller issues to those with basic skills means the bigger problems get to the true specialists more quickly.

Having students serve in this capacity not only reduces a school's overall need for support and keeps things running smoothly, it also builds the students' self-efficacy and leadership skills. "Last year some of these kids would barely speak," Sanders observes. "Now they're giving presentations to big crowds of people."

One unexpected result of putting the support team in place has been its impact on the student body. "I find that teachers still generally come to me for help, but the students now go to each other," says Sanders. While some school tech support models focus on training teachers, Sanders chose to have his team put most of their energy on teaching their peers.

He likens their work to that of a "force multiplier," a military term that refers to any tool or factor that, when added to a force, makes that force significantly more effective than it would be without it, "multiplying" its impact. With the help of these student experts, the school is growing together in their technology skills. "You know it's working because no one's asking for help," Sanders says, "or they just bypass the system altogether and go straight to each other."

The students in your building are walking around with skills— or the *capacity* for skills—that your school needs, especially when it comes to technology. Regardless of how formally or informally you structure their assistance, if you start considering students as potential *resources*, if you start thinking of the ways they can authentically contribute to your learning community as teachers in their own right, you have already shifted in the right direction.

HACK 6

MARIGOLD COMMITTEES

Nurture New Teachers with a Circle of Mentors

If you want to lift yourself up, lift someone else.
— BOOKER T. WASHINGTON

THE PROBLEM: POOR TEACHER RETENTION

IT'S NO SECRET that teacher retention is a huge issue for schools. According to most estimates, about a third of new teachers leave the profession within the first three years, and about half leave within the first five. This creates a vicious cycle of wasted time as schools must look for, interview, hire, and train new teachers every year. And because inexperienced teachers need several years to develop the skills of excellent teaching, schools with significant retention problems have little hope of ever realizing excellence for their students.

Although some school districts have mentoring programs in place for new teachers, the effectiveness of these programs is inconsistent: Many formal mentoring programs require so much paperwork and scheduled observations, they may not have room for the kind of natural relationship-building necessary for true mentoring to occur. In other cases, lack of accountability on the part of the mentor results in little or no interaction between mentor and mentee. And many schools have no plan for mentoring whatsoever: New teachers find supportive role models by luck, or not at all.

This problem is further compounded by the fact that many teachers in their early years are reluctant to ask for help. They know everyone in the building is incredibly busy, so they hold back their requests and questions, not wanting to bother anyone.

> Many teachers, including new ones, are fiercely independent and do not like asking for help, even when they desperately need it.

Ego also plays a role: The new teacher, wanting to appear capable and worthy of the position they have just been given, too often feigns perfect calm, even if inside they are kind of a mess. Instead of reaching out for support, some new teachers keep their struggles private, bottling them up every day until the day they start looking for a new career.

If current mentoring programs worked as well as they could, fewer teachers would be leaving the profession. What we need is a different kind of mentoring for new teachers.

THE HACK: ESTABLISH A YEAR-LONG WELCOMING COMMITTEE FOR NEW TEACHERS

Every school has a few teachers who have that "it" factor: They love their work, they love the students, and they never seem to run out of enthusiasm. Their very presence inspires others. Many of these same teachers are also naturally good mentors, but if new teachers don't happen to be formally assigned to them, or find them in some other way, those new teachers will never benefit from the support and wisdom that could be gained from consistently spending time with these motivating teachers.

If these teachers formed a group that met regularly with all new or less-experienced teachers (or any teacher who needs support) to talk, exchange ideas, solve problems, and share stories, the important mentor-mentee relationships would naturally form. From meeting with these groups, rookie teachers would pick up tips, grow more comfortable in sharing their questions and concerns, and begin to develop mindsets that resemble those of their mentors. In groups like these, new teachers would develop a love of teaching and problems would be addressed early, before they had time to develop into career-ending disasters. We call these groups Marigold Committees.

When gardeners want to protect young, vulnerable plants, especially tomatoes, they will often plant marigolds nearby. The marigold emits chemicals that protect other plants from worms, animals, and disease, thereby nurturing their growth. Similarly, certain teachers can serve the same purpose as marigolds to new teachers, encircling them in positive energy and helping them fend off the negativity that can often poison a beginning teacher. This concept was originally introduced on the Cult of Pedagogy blog in a post entitled "Find Your Marigold: The One Essential Rule for New Teachers."

Gardeners are advised not to limit this proactive planting to just one or two plants: To achieve best results, marigolds should be planted in clusters all over a garden. If the Marigold teachers in your building form themselves into a committee, their protective, nurturing power will explode.

✦ WHAT **YOU** CAN DO TOMORROW ✦

It may take several years to gather just the right mix of dedicated teachers for a strong Marigold Committee, but there's no time like the present to get things started.

- **Start small**. If you are an experienced teacher who would like to form your own Marigold Committee, find at least one other like-minded teacher and together, invite at least one new (or newish) teacher to meet with you; this can be going out for a snack after school, having lunch together in one of your classrooms, or even setting up a Voxer group (see Hack 1). Explain that you'd like to talk about how things have been going.

- **Have a Q & A session**. In preparation for your get-together, ask the new teacher to jot down a few notes about his or her current needs or questions, and bring the notes when you meet.

- **Recruit a Marigold**. If you are an administrator, approach your most positive teacher about starting a Marigold Committee, and brainstorm a list of other teachers who might be interested in serving in this capacity.

A BLUEPRINT FOR FULL IMPLEMENTATION

Step 1: Establish your committee.

After explaining the concept of a Marigold Committee to the staff, offer the opportunity to anyone who would like to serve on it. Although the committee does not have to have a formal leader, if membership is large—more than 5 or 6 people—designating a facilitator or chair would be a smart idea so someone is in charge of planning events and keeping everyone informed.

Should an administrator serve on the committee? Since the Marigold Committee is a new concept, there are no hard-and-fast rules, but the presence of an administrator may alter the collegial feel you're going for. New teachers are likely to have questions they may not want an administrator to hear, questions like, "If I want to take a sick day, but I'm not *actually* sick, is it okay to just say so, or do I have to pretend?"

Step 2: Survey new teachers.

Figure out what new teachers need by conducting a survey to learn about their concerns and questions. This survey should ideally be given in written or online form, rather than in person, to allow teachers time to reflect and offer honest responses. Most of your survey should consist of open-ended questions like these:

- What are you struggling with right now?

- What do you need information about?

- What questions do you have about our school? About our administration? About our students? About teaching in general?

Because new teachers don't necessarily know what they don't know, also provide some checklist-type or multiple-choice questions to help them consider other areas where they might need help. For example, "Which of these topics would you like to learn more about?" followed by a list of topics like classroom management, curriculum requirements, getting classroom materials, technology, setting up your retirement/financial plan, and the teachers' union.

Step 3: Strategize.

When survey results come in, meet with other committee members to plan how to address the new teachers' concerns. What issues are the most common among many of the newcomers? Is there someone on the committee with specialized skills or knowledge who can help someone solve a specific problem right away? Would other topics be most appropriate for whole-group discussion? What resources should the committee gather to support the new teachers? Whatever you do, use the survey to guide your interactions with the newcomers, rather than assuming you know what they need.

Also, consider how often you might want to meet. Will your committee hold monthly gatherings, do something once a week, or just meet once per quarter? Although it's smart to plan based on everyone's needs rather than stick to a rigid schedule, scheduling a few gatherings early on will build strong relationships that will last throughout the year.

Step 4: Hold your first gathering.

Keep this light, fun, and informal. New teachers are feeling a lot of anxiety, and if the first gathering is overly formal—more like an interview than a party—it will only increase that anxiety. Remember that although the Marigold Committee exists to share information, its main purpose is to build relationships with new teachers. Here are some suggestions for a first get-together:

- Feed everyone. Whether it's sandwiches at lunch, snacks after school, or a full dinner, make sure there's food.

- Set aside time for each Marigold to share a short reflection about his or her first year of teaching. Because the new teachers don't know the Marigolds well, they haven't developed the necessary trust to share what's really bothering them. That trust can grow quickly if the Marigolds show some vulnerability from the start and share stories that reveal the truth about teaching: Everyone's first year is hard.

- Plan an equal amount of time to let the newcomers talk. Although the Marigolds' sharing is necessary to build relationships, do not allow it to dominate the first gathering, or newcomers will quickly see the committee as unconcerned about their needs. Give the new teachers an opportunity to ask questions and share their concerns.

- Keep things moving. A whole-group discussion may be too awkward at first, especially if people don't know each other well. To get the conversation going, pair people up to discuss different questions or play some other kind of conversation-starting game to loosen the group up and get them talking.

Step 5: Continue gathering in a variety of ways.

For future gatherings, offer some variety, experimenting with meeting times, lengths, and activities, so you don't tax anyone's schedule and you offer different paths for connection. Here are some options to consider:

- Create opportunities for one-on-one interactions. Not all personalities will click, and if your gatherings always bring the whole group together, a personality clash may prevent some new teachers from opening up and getting the help they need. Look for ways to create individual connections as well. Committee members might choose individual newcomers to make direct, one-on-one contact with on a regular basis.

- Offer brief, informal workshops or presentations given by individual Marigolds on areas of expertise: satisfying IEP requirements, making calls to or meeting with parents, behavior management strategies, or using the school's grading system.

- Short, quick gatherings—like a 15-minute doughnut party before school—can go a long way toward recon- necting the newcomers with their Marigolds and starting conversations that can continue later on.

Step 6: Follow up. Then follow up some more.

Many teachers, including new ones, are fiercely independent and do not like asking for help, even when they desperately need it. So it's up to the mentors to stay in touch, to go beyond passing in the hall and saying, "If you need anything, just ask." Instead, ask specific questions that will generate more detailed conversations: "How are things going with classroom management? How late are you staying every day? What are you teaching right now?" If you show a genuine interest and regularly demonstrate availability, the new teachers will feel more comfortable coming to you for help.

Step 7: Reflect.

When the year is coming to a close, ask the newcomers to reflect and share their thoughts on what was most helpful and offer suggestions for improvement or enhancement for the following year's cohort of new teachers.

OVERCOMING PUSHBACK

Even an idea as simple and positive as this can have some possible obstacles. Here are ways to address them:

There's no time. The nice thing about this hack is that it doesn't nec- essarily require lots of time. Unlike a formal mentoring system that has paperwork and scheduled observations, Marigold Committees are informal, social, and require no paperwork. So if no one wants to take this on due to the potential time commitment, make it efficient:

Even if you just hold a single event early in the year, you will plant the seed for better collaboration and mentorship.

If teachers aren't compensated for mentoring, they won't do it. Every school has some teachers who take great satisfaction in helping other teachers learn the craft. If no one is willing to form an actual committee, you might want to start by having a few teachers simply identify themselves as Marigolds and introduce themselves at the first faculty meeting.

Mentee teachers will feel inferior or embarrassed. Like teacher visits using a Pineapple Chart (Hack 2), it's important to be transparent from the start about the intention of Marigold Committees. Remind teachers that the committees are designed to build camaraderie, a sense of belonging, and a strong community of outstanding educators. Marigolds aren't know-it-alls; they are friends and mentors.

THE HACK IN ACTION

Barbara LaBarre, a chemistry teacher at Binghamton High School in Binghamton, New York, started the first Marigold Committee (and coined the term) as part of her school's improvement plan for the 2014-2015 school year.

"I had read the 'Find Your Marigold' article and loved it so much I printed it out and shared it with my principal when we were writing our school improvement plan," LaBarre explains. "Our school is large and can be daunting for a young new teacher, so I asked my principal if we could start a 'Marigold Committee' to welcome the teachers and help them settle in, learn the ropes and generally feel more comfortable in their new school."

After recruiting several other interested teachers, the newly formed committee held two luncheons for the new teachers, where the veteran teachers shared tips and resources. "Things they would not normally get in a training," LaBarre says, "common sense stuff like bring your plan and attendance book out of the building with you during a fire drill, how to get needed furniture and supplies for your room, and what is expected of you in observations."

After the two luncheons, the mentors remained available to offer support on a more informal basis. To help new teachers identify Marigolds in Binghamton's large, four-story building, the art teacher on the committee made felt marigold pins, and committee members wore them to the luncheons and some faculty meetings.

"The group has created relationships that may not have developed otherwise," LaBarre says, noting that new teachers have felt comfortable approaching her seeking help with classroom management and offering to co-sponsor activities for the upcoming school year. And getting together for Marigold gatherings had the unexpected effect of bonding the new teachers with each other. "The new teachers made a little cohort of their own," she explains, "once they knew who they all were!"

Principal Roxie Oberg says Binghamton plans to expand on the Committee's work in the future. "I believe it is critical to support our newer teachers, not just for the first year, but all the way through the tenure process and beyond," she says. "In that way, we will grow mentors who will be able to support the next generation of teachers and continue to develop a collegial, supportive teaching community."

Supporting new teachers doesn't require an expensive, complicated program. To help a new teacher grow, you don't need tons of forms and bullet points for observations. Those things help, but at the start of the emotional, difficult, and often maddening journey of teaching, there is no substitute for relationships. A Marigold Committee could be the thing that keeps your teachers with you, growing and learning and looking forward to another great school year.

THE IN-CLASS FLIP

Bypass the Hurdles of Flipped Learning by Keeping It in School

If you run into a wall, don't turn around and give up.
Figure out how to climb it, go through it, or work around it.
— MICHAEL JORDAN, BASKETBALL PLAYER AND ENTREPRENEUR

THE PROBLEM: FLIPPED LEARNING
CAN FALL APART AT HOME

FLIPPED LEARNING HAS become wildly popular in education. Unlike a traditional course setup, where content is delivered in class and students apply and practice their learning through homework, the flipped classroom turns that arrangement on its head: The initial content delivery happens at home (often through a video of some sort), and then students and teachers re-converge in class to apply and practice their learning.

The thinking behind this arrangement is that teachers' expertise is much more valuable during that application stage; when content is delivered in an automated format, this frees up the teacher to really interact with students as they use and engage with the content through discussion, practice, role-play and simulation, inquiry, and hands-on projects.

Here's the thing, though: If a lesson is going to flip with any success, the at-home learning absolutely has to happen. Students *must* learn the initial content in order to apply it. This requires every student to have at home a working device, a reliable, consistent Internet connection, and an environment conducive to concentration. Unfortunately, in many communities, securing all three can be challenging. Even in cases when all of these things can be arranged, their stability can be questionable.

For some teachers, these complications have been enough to make them abandon flipping altogether. They quickly write off flipped learning as a trend that just doesn't work or isn't worth the trouble. This is a shame, because in too many cases, these teachers resign themselves to staying in the role of *content provider*, allowing their time to be consumed with lecture and demonstration when it could be better spent engaging directly with students.

What if you and your students could still get the benefits of flipped learning without messing with all the variables of the home environment? What if the whole flipped process could remain in school?

THE HACK: "FLIP" YOUR CLASS...IN CLASS

The In-Class Flip moves the flipped learning model inside the walls of your classroom. Using a set of iPads, tablets, a few classroom computers, or even students' own devices, the content delivery portion of a lesson—the "home" part in a true flip—would be set up as a station in the classroom. This allows students to receive the content in the same way that they would at home, while freeing up the teacher to engage remaining students as they apply the learning from the video *or* from previous lessons.

To demonstrate, let's assume a teacher has a 10-minute recorded video lesson to deliver some portion of his content, and his classroom has six tablets for student use. He sets those tablets up as one station (with earbuds for non-disruptive listening) and arranges to have the 10-minute video accessible through those tablets.

Next, he sets up a station where students will *directly apply the concepts introduced in the video*, such as a writing assignment, a set of discussion cards, a game, or a practice sheet. Students will go to this station only after they have seen the video. Because he has 24 students, but only six tablets, the teacher needs more stations, so he sets up three more that do not rely on the information from the video. These can be short hands-on activities, skills practices, games, or reviews of prior learning.

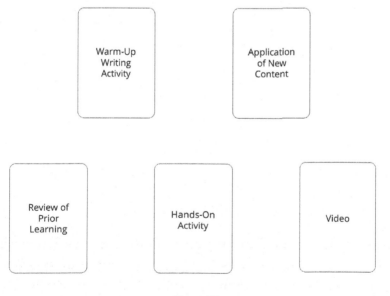

Figure 7-1

When students arrive, they are divided into groups of six and placed at the first four stations. Note that station 5, which students can only do *after* they have watched the video, stays empty for the first round.

For the following round, students rotate to the next station. This time, the first group of students watching the video is able to apply that content in the next station. Although stations 1 through 3 are just basic classroom activities, the rotation from station 4 to station 5 in this example is basically what replicates a flip.

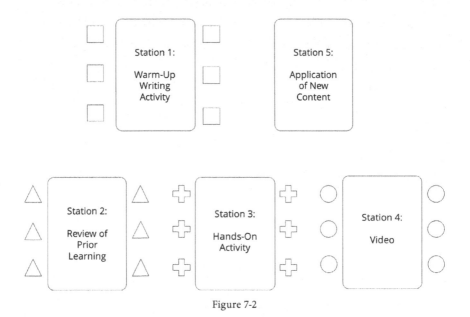

Figure 7-2

Instead of delivering the new content himself, this teacher now has station 4 to do it for him. This frees him up to rotate around to the other stations, interacting with students as they engage with both the new content at Station 5 *and* prior learning at Stations 1 through 3.

WHAT YOU CAN DO TOMORROW

Although setting up an In-Class Flip requires planning and preparation, you can get a taste of how it works by trying this mini-version:

- **Go on a treasure hunt.** Locate a video online that delivers some simple piece of content related to your subject area—something you haven't taught yet. If YouTube isn't an option at your school, try looking at Vimeo, TED-Ed, or TeacherTube.

- **Prepare a post-video activity.** Create some kind of task students can do after they have viewed the video—a written assignment, a quiz, discussion questions, something hands-on—that will require application of the learning from the video.

- **Prepare another independent activity.** This task should not be directly related to or dependent upon the video in any way. It is not necessary to create a full set of stations for the "non-flipped" time; as long as you assign independent work that will engage the rest of the class while other students rotate through the flip, the class should run smoothly.

- **Complete a test run.** As part of tomorrow's class, have students take turns sitting at the video viewing station, then completing the post-video task. Make yourself available to answer questions during the task. Instruct students who are not watching the video or have not yet seen it to do the independent activity during the remaining time.

A BLUEPRINT FOR FULL IMPLEMENTATION

Step 1: Take inventory.

Determine how many reliable classroom devices you have access to on a regular basis. These do not all have to be the same kind; a combination of tablets, laptops, desktop computers, and even smartphones would work—anything that allows students to view pre-recorded videos, either through an Internet connection or by storing the videos on the devices themselves. If you are very short on devices—say, you only have two—consider whether students might be able to pair up on the same device at the same time. Headphone splitters can be purchased for less than $5, allowing you to plug two sets of headphones into the same output jack.

Step 2: Choose lessons to flip.

Decide what portion of the content will be delivered through video. Although video is not the *only* way to deliver content in a flip, it is the most common, so we'll use that in our discussion here. The content should be something students can grasp reasonably well on their own. It could be a short lesson that explains a new concept and gives examples, a demonstration of a hands-on task they will do later, or the steps of a skill they will practice after the video is done. Students will only be able to absorb small amounts of content in one stretch, so consider how you will break up the content, providing stops during the video for students to take notes, answer comprehension questions, or briefly practice skills.

Step 3: Record the lessons, or find pre-made videos online.

This is the time-consuming part. If you want to start by looking for videos created by others, consider the libraries offered on sites like EDpuzzle, eduCanon, and TED-Ed. If you are unable to find videos that meet your specific needs—and for many people, this is the case—you'll need to start making your own. Creating these videos is easier than you think: One way to do it is to build a presentation using PowerPoint or Google Slides, then present it in slideshow mode while you talk, recording the whole thing using screencasting software like Screencast-O-Matic, Jing, or ShowMe.

Step 4: Store your videos for student access.

The easiest way to do this is to create your own YouTube channel, upload the videos there, then share the links with students or embed the videos in a class website. If YouTube is not an option, videos can be uploaded and shared via a cloud-based system like Google Drive or Screencast.com. Of course, if you are an iOS user, it's easy to simply share anything you create directly from your device. With literally a couple of clicks or swipes, content from your iPhone, Mac or iPad can be shared wirelessly from your screen to your students' devices. This makes flipping your videos in class astonishingly simple.

Step 5: Set up your viewing station.

Arrange devices in one general area of your classroom—a table, a collection of desks, or designate a few computer stations. Include written instructions for how students should access the video for that lesson, what to do when they are finished, and some general troubleshooting tips. If you want students to take notes as they watch the video, include instructions for that as well.

Step 6: Set up the other stations.

You will need one station for direct application of the content in the video, then a few more for students to visit when they are not viewing the video or applying the video content. To figure out how many you need, consider how many students can view the video at one time—that could be one station. However many students you have at the viewing station is the same number you can have at every other station. Remember to add one additional station, to be left empty in the first round, where students will apply the learning they did in the viewing station.

In the example we talked about earlier, the teacher had six devices and 24 students. If all stations were going to be used during every rotation, he would only need four stations—one for each group of six. But *because students can't use station 5 without viewing the video first,* that has to be left empty in round 1. Therefore, the activity requires five total stations, not four.

Step 7: Train students.

In order for your stations to run smoothly, students need to understand how they work. Show students what's expected of them at each station, what they should do if they finish early, and how you will signal for a rotation. To establish clear guidelines for appropriate use of the devices, consider your answers to the following questions:

- Are students allowed to leave the video screen if they finish before it's time to rotate?

- What other sites/applications are okay to visit?

- What should students do if they want to re-watch a section of the video?

- How should students conduct themselves within and between the stations?

Step 8: Evaluate and Iterate.

After your first attempt, when some things have inevitably not gone as planned, evaluate what you might need to do differently the next time around. Did some activities take too long, messing up the flow from station to station? Did some stations require more troubleshooting from you, rather than meaningful engagement? Did the station after the video really delve into that content, or could you do better? Ask students for their feedback, reminding them that the goal is to give them more interaction with the content, and with you. And keep in mind that establishing this new model will take some time to get right, but if it ultimately allows you and your students to learn more deeply, it's worth it.

OVERCOMING PUSHBACK

This is nothing new; it's called blended learning. Think of the In-Class Flip as a *subset* of blended learning, a more specific instructional plan that falls under the blended learning umbrella. Blended learning is a general approach to instruction, where teachers combine traditional, face-to-face instruction with online resources, which can include videos, websites, backchannel discussions, and online courses. As long as the method combines online learning and traditional instruction, it qualifies as blended learning.

The In-Class Flip narrows this broad definition into one specific configuration, where station rotation sets up a sequence that mimics the flipped learning experience and teachers select "flipped materials" with the *deliberate goal of replacing face-to-face content delivery* in order to free up time for deeper exploration of the material.

I don't have time to make my own videos. Finding just-right videos takes time, and yes, creating them takes even more. As with any other skill, you'll find that this process takes much longer the first few times you do it, but that you'll get faster the more you practice.

Start small and simple, with topics that are easy to teach and don't require long, complex videos. Give yourself permission to create "good enough" videos—if you insist on beautiful, professionally edited productions, they will indeed take forever to create, so go easy on yourself. And remember that the time you spend creating the videos now will be returned to you over and over again as you re-use the videos in future years.

I thought the purpose of flipping was to create more class time for engagement with the teacher; if you play the videos during class, don't you still lose that time? Yes, to some degree, and that's what makes this more of a hack, because the content delivery takes away some class time, it can't offer *all* of the advantages of a true flip. However, it does provide some things a true flip doesn't: It allows for greater supervision, increasing the chances that students are actually accessing the content, something that's harder to measure when it's done at home. The teacher's proximity makes it possible for students to ask clarifying questions if they need to. At home, if a student gets hung up on one small issue two minutes into a video, they may spend the remaining 10 minutes feeling confused; with the teacher nearby, they can ask a quick question and get a lot more out of the video. It provides excellent training for a true flip.

Once students get used to the cycle of flipped learning, once they learn how to access the videos and complete whatever work is required to go along with them, once they understand that they must demonstrate comprehension of that content in the follow-up activity, they will be better prepared to participate in a true flip that sends that learning home.

I hate relying on technology; something always goes wrong. This is a legitimate concern. The risk for tech-related problems can be minimized in three ways: (1) Do a test run before trying it with your students. Always open up a few of the individual devices before launching a lesson to make sure they can access the video. (2) Have a backup plan. Consider ahead of time what you can do if the video simply doesn't work as planned — whether it's to have an alternate activity ready or a written passage that delivers the same content, albeit in a less dynamic format. (3) Keep a helper on call. Let the "tech people" in your building know when you'll be flipping, so they can try to stay as available and reachable as they can. (Don't have enough "tech people" in your building? Take a look at Hack 5: Student Tech Gurus.)

THE HACK IN ACTION

Mark Levezow, a 5th grade literacy and social studies teacher at Omro Elementary School in Omro, Wisconsin, uses this kind of configuration with his students. "Because I work in a rural district," Levezow says, "many of the students either don't have devices or Internet access." By flipping part of his lesson in class, he can still take advantage of pre-recorded lessons without having to rely on at-home technology.

"I use Google Classroom as my hub," he explains. "My mini-lesson videos are captured via Screencast-O-Matic, and then they are uploaded to my school YouTube account. From there, I use eduCanon to embed questions into the videos. Responses are automatically assessed by edu-Canon. I then use the assessment results to see where misconceptions or misunderstandings are occurring. I reteach in small groups, or have students re-watch the video. The blended aspect of our daily routines is only one of four centers during literacy and social studies."

While Levezow admits that creating the videos is time-consuming and his classroom technology isn't perfect, he is still a big fan. "It has freed up time for me, so I can work in small groups with the students who need it. And the students love it—they seem motivated to get on their Chromebooks and view the lessons."

When we try something new and it doesn't work, it can be tempting to abandon the idea altogether and return to what we're used to. But with a little adjustment and creativity, we can distill the essence of a new approach and still find ways to make it work for us. Flipped learning—in its purest form, or even in this adaptation—gives teachers more time to engage with their students and the content. That's a goal worth working toward.

THE BOOK NOOK

Create a Culture of Readers at Your School with Free Books for Everyone

The things I want to know are in books; my best
friend is the man who'll get me a book I ain't read.
—ABRAHAM LINCOLN

THE PROBLEM: NONREADERS

IN 2014, THE United Nations Educational Scientific and Cultural Organization (UNESCO) reported that 121 million youths around the world can't read. Combining this number with the almost 800 million adults who are functionally illiterate reveals a staggering fact—nearly one-seventh of the world's population can't read or write. As shocking as these statistics are, most policymakers and education leaders are, indeed, aware of them; the move to improve reading achievement has grown exponentially over the past few decades.

Still, the frightening number of non-readers doesn't appear to be shrinking, which is equally surprising, because there are hundreds, perhaps thousands, of programs aimed at improving reading achievement.

So why do our children continue to *not* read? One answer to this important question is simple: They don't read because they don't have access to books. In most cases, this is an issue related to poverty. Low-income families typically don't have many books in their homes, and many live in communities without good libraries. Hacking poverty is something we won't attempt here, but we can all hack this unacceptable reading problem: All it takes is a room and some books.

THE HACK: BUILD A BOOK NOOK

Some K-12 buildings have bookstores, much like colleges have. These are places where students can purchase basic school supplies, along with young adult book series, graphic novels, and other popular works of fiction and nonfiction. Like the bookstore, a Book Nook contains books, but they are not for sale; they are free to all students. A Book Nook is any designated space in the school where books are available for free—not to borrow, not to buy, but *to take*. There is no check-out or check-in system. When a student takes a book, it's his to keep for as long as he likes.

The brilliance of the Book Nook, or any designated room created to house giveaway books for students, is that it promotes reading by simply putting books in kids' hands. Often, these are students who might not have books of their own. As literacy expert Stephen Krashen has noted in many papers and speeches, reluctant readers become reluctant because they do not have access to books. The Book Nook is one way to solve this problem.

✸✸ WHAT **YOU** CAN DO TOMORROW ✸✸

It's difficult to argue with the simplicity and philosophy behind the Book Nook, but there are obvious challenges to starting one. With a little ingenuity and a lot of perseverance, you can have the beginnings of a nearly self-sustaining Book Nook as early as tomorrow. Try these basic steps before diving headlong into this project:

- **Bring books to school.** We're betting you thought the first step would be to locate a room for your Book Nook. Sure, this is a reasonable starting ground, but choosing a room may not, in many cases, be a step you can take tomorrow. Deciding on a room may require time and planning, but it only takes one visionary educator to collect some books, bring them to school, and give them to kids. Start by culling the shelves in your own home library. This strategy proved to be strikingly effective for the teachers at Knapp Elementary School, as we illustrate later in this chapter. Ask neighbors for some giveaways for your students; it's such an easy request; who wouldn't want to contribute to this amazing cause? Contact your colleagues, friends, and your students' parents via social media or your classroom website or blog and ask them to bring any appropriate books that they're willing to donate to school.

- **Plant the first seed in a single classroom.** As you plan full implementation of a Book Nook for your school, create a small-scale nook in your own classroom. Show your students the collection of books you brought from home and from friends and share the amazing idea you have for a free book room. Be sure your students understand that the Book Nook is not a library; books in the nook are theirs to keep.

➤ **Give students books to handle.** Even if you aren't able to grab enough books at first to give one to every student, encourage them to browse your small collection. Invite them to touch the books, preview them, turn the pages, smell them, and read a few pages. Preach the value of books and of reading. "We are a culture of readers" should be your mantra.

➤ **Make homework finding a book to donate.** If ever there were a useful homework assignment, this is it. When you launch your Book Nook, throw out your standard homework assignment that day and ask students to embark on a treasure hunt for books. Challenge them to bring at least one book, which they are willing to donate, to class the next day. If you're a math teacher, your students will love this homework assignment, because most don't equate math to reading. And yes, math teachers can build book nooks filled with math-related and other wonderful content.

A BLUEPRINT FOR FULL IMPLEMENTATION

Step 1: Build a team.

Successful book nooks are created and loved by people who are more passionate about reading than almost anything. Find book lovers and invite them to be part of this fantastic project. Team members don't have to be English teachers, but they must be dedicated go-getters who absolutely love books. Important players include, but are not limited to, your school librarian, an involved parent, at least one student leader, a community business owner or manager, a representative from your local library or bookstore, and anyone else you believe is skilled at organizing people and projects. If no one on your staff is willing or able to step up and be in charge, but you really want to see the Book Nook come to life, consider whether one key staff member's responsibilities might be reduced to free up some time to manage your nook.

> Places like Starbucks and Barnes & Noble draw readers in because they are cozy and hip.

Step 2: Find your nook.

Most schools don't have spare rooms available for this kind of project, so be creative: Your nook could be a large closet, an alcove in a hallway, or even a shelf that runs the length of a classroom. When you read the "Hack in Action" section later, you'll see it really can be done anywhere.

Step 3: Brand it.

Places like Starbucks and Barnes & Noble draw readers in because they are cozy and hip. If you set up your Book Nook with this in mind, branding it as a place built for all kids—cool, nerdy, quirky, studious, and athletic—you'll attract more students. In a perfect world, your nook would be designed for lingering, complete with comfortable chairs, couches, bean bags, and maybe a vending machine, rather than a grab-and-go storeroom with a few shelves of books. You might even hold a contest to have students name your Book Nook, furthering its branding and getting more buy-in from the student body. With thoughtful packaging, you send the message that if you haven't been to the nook lately you're missing out.

Step 4: Find benefactors.

You don't need millionaires to create a self-sustaining hub for giveaway books, but a few well-chosen benefactors are a must. These are often people who have access to books. One of your team members should visit the local library and explain how they can help. Libraries cull their collections regularly; most of the time they sell books they're eliminating as a fundraiser. Once librarians understand what you're doing, they'll likely be willing to give books to a school, rather than sell them at 25 cents apiece. Make the person donating the books feel like an important part of the culture of readers you're creating, and she'll be more inclined to give you books throughout the year.

> Your first goal is to acquire books by the hundreds. Books by the thousands.

Don't forget other entrepreneurs in your community. Find as many small businesses as possible and ask the owners to contribute yearly to the cause. They can purchase books and bring them periodically, or they can simply write you a check.

Step 5: Manage the Nook.

Without a proper management system, your Book Nook is doomed to fail, even if you have a glorious room with more books than the Library of Congress. Set some guidelines (neatness, behavior, max number of students browsing at one time or number of books that can be taken in a day) and post them prominently. While this is not a swap meet, students should always feel encouraged to give back to the room.

You don't need a Dewey Decimal System, but there should be some semblance of organization. Create clearly labeled sections by genre. You can decide if you want to organize by author name, title, or subject. You may feel it's not necessary to maintain any alphabetical or numerical system, which is fine. Regardless of the method you adopt, be sure it is maintained. Use everyone on the team to manage the nook. If it becomes an overwhelming chore, it won't last.

Step 6: Invite students and teachers to the nook.

This isn't *Field of Dreams*; just because you build it doesn't mean they'll come. We're talking about books, not baseball, and the sad truth is that many kids hate reading, primarily because they've never owned books. The nook can change this attitude, but it will only happen if all shareholders believe in it. Your team should create a system that encourages teachers to organize "field trips" to the nook.

Step 7: Promote, promote, promote.

Snap pictures of students giving and taking books from the nook. Shoot video of students reading; share these assets on your school website, on Facebook, on Instagram, and any other website or social network that contains school information. With every picture, video, or blurb about the nook, ask for more books. Finding and donating books will become contagious, and soon you'll have dozens of people constantly contributing to your cause.

Step 8: Always Be Collecting.

People in sales live by the rule of ABC (Always Be Closing). Use your own ABC rule to stock your shelves. You and all stakeholders at your school are now collectors. Books are your lifeblood, so be pushy about collecting them.

Teach students to scavenge, providing a list of great places to find used books: Friends, relatives, yard sales, used bookstores, and the local library are excellent places to find free books. All staff members should constantly be on the lookout for books. Remind your friends and family members that you always need fiction and non-fiction books. Take everything; never turn down a book thinking it's not right for the Nook or is not age appropriate. The management team can cull the collection. Your first goal is to acquire books by the hundreds. Books by the thousands.

Step 9: Give it to students.

When your team has the Book Nook running on autopilot (this might take a year or two), turn the operation over to students. This might be tough in elementary school, but teens should be able to handle it if properly coached. Explain to students that the Book Nook is theirs, and they need to make it a success.

OVERCOMING PUSHBACK

It's too late for our non-reading teens. It's never too late. Sure, teaching a high school student who reads on a third-grade level requires more than simply handing him a book, but that book is the most critical first step to becoming a lifelong reader. Bring non-readers to the nook and help them browse. Talk about what excites them, and find it. When you hand them books and say, "It's yours to keep," they'll want to read. Be sure to follow up with other necessary interventions, because if they struggle, they may not come back.

Isn't this just a second library? The best Book Nooks resemble libraries, because they're filled with hundreds, hopefully thousands, of books in all genres. Remember, the magic of the Book Nook, what distinguishes it from the library, is that the books are not loaned. They are gifts.

You make it sound easy, but isn't this really a major undertaking? Yes, it's a major undertaking, for sure. The hacks in this book solve problems with simple ideas, and giving away books is definitely this. Most simple, life-changing programs, though, take dedication and hard work. However, with the right team and support from a few key players, this might be the most rewarding hard work you ever do. In many schools, teachers organize the prom, coach the robotics team, and run the yearbook for no additional pay. These co-curricular activities often become the best part of their daily work lives. People who coordinate Book

Nooks aren't just collectors; they encourage kids to be lifelong readers, and this undertaking becomes a crucial part of their lives.

THE HACK IN ACTION

Before he began working full time in education at the University of Pennsylvania, Joe Mazza was a principal at Knapp Elementary School in Philadelphia. Mazza and a few teachers at Knapp believed that many students do not read because they don't have access to books. "We all know that the amount of books in a child's home has a direct correlation to their reading level and how jacked up they are about reading," Mazza says. "So we really wanted to help kids have books in their homes."

Mazza assisted a small team of stakeholders that included teachers, parents and staff members on the School Climate Committee. They met, discussed the problem, and brainstormed ways to bring books to Knapp's students. "A lot of us had books at our houses that were just going to waste. We wondered how many others had the same experience, and we put out a challenge to send in books." The community answered the team's challenge in a big way, as Knapp amassed over 4,000 books in just a few months. When that giant collection dwindled, the team reached out to Scholastic, and the publishing giant provided roughly 2,000 more books that the school could add to its shelves and pass on to hungry readers.

There were so many books, in fact, that Mazza and his team had to choose some unorthodox places to put them. They placed bookshelves in the main lobby (this made it easy for parents to drop off books they wanted to donate), around the gymnasium where evening events took place, and in another high-traffic hallway. "We didn't care if the books came back," Mazza explains. "We just wanted to get books in the hands of kids." At the end of the school year, the team divided books into various reading levels and sent students home with backpacks full of them, so they could continue reading during summer break.

Knapp's Book Nooks not only created a culture of readers, they helped bring the school community together. "They became a hangout," according to Mazza. "They opened up a lot of doors for a lot of different people. Between the constant give-take and equipping kids with summer books, it was something that really gave the community an opportunity to contribute. It was a really powerful experience."

Are you frustrated by a culture of nonreaders at your school? Perhaps you've tried virtually every reading intervention and tutorial program available. Still, many kids don't read, and there's nothing more frustrating. Before you pull out one more hair or furrow another eyebrow in frustration, ask yourself this one simple question: What do our nonreaders need that we're not providing? Consider this simple hack; then, go get them some books, and build a culture of readers at your school. Oh, and don't forget to smile, knowing that you are changing the world.

THE GLASS CLASSROOM

Put Learning on Display with Social Media

Transparency is not the same as looking
straight through a building: It's not just a
physical idea, it's also an intellectual one.
— HELMUT JAHN, GERMAN ARCHITECT

THE PROBLEM: WHAT HAPPENS IN CLASS STAYS IN CLASS

WE TEACH BEHIND walls. These walls block everyone's view: parents, colleagues, administrators, and other students. When we set up a demonstration, deliver new and exciting content, or give students instructions, these experiences stay between us and the students who happen to be in our room at the precise time when the experiences happen.

Sure, they might take notes. We might provide handouts or links to supplementary information, but the real, live experiences float away as soon as they're over. The ephemeral nature of our teaching, the fact that what we do in our classrooms is more or less shrouded, contributes to problems like these:

- Parents who are expected to support their child with homework assignments or projects often throw up their hands, not fully understanding our intention with a given assignment, or misdirect the child to complete a task according to their own interpretation of it.

- Absent students, even when given make-up work, can never quite replicate the experience of being in class.

- Our collaboration with other teachers is almost always limited to our *description of what we do*, rather than being able to actually show what goes on in our classrooms. Even if we take advantage of Pineapple Charts (see Hack 2), we are still limited to observing the teachers in our building, by the constraints of our individual schedules, and by our own comfort with approaching other people about their classroom practices.

> With social media and other mobile apps, we can fully share our classroom activities with others, effectively making our walls transparent.

What if we could tear down the walls of our classrooms and make our in-class learning activities transparent to anyone who's interested?

THE HACK: BUILD A TRANSPARENT CLASSROOM WITH SOCIAL MEDIA

For four months in 1915, education pioneer Maria Montessori installed a glass-walled classroom right in the middle of San Francisco's Panama Pacific International Exposition. She wanted visitors to see children at work in a classroom using the

Montessori method, a pedagogical approach that had yet to take hold in the United States. The response was phenomenal: The classroom drew crowds of onlookers; many returned day after day for repeat visits. Newspapers covered the event, and the new approach soon gained traction in America. Even today, some Montessori schools install temporary Glass Classrooms in storefronts and parks to give the general public an up-close look at how their methods work.

A century later, technology allows us to achieve the same goal of sharing our classroom practices without the expense or hassle of constructing actual glass walls. With social media and other mobile apps, we can fully share our classroom activities with others, effectively making our walls transparent. Whether it's parents, other students, colleagues, community members, or curious educators from anywhere at all, anyone can experience the learning activities you want to share.

With a class Twitter, Facebook, or Instagram account, you and your students can share photos, status updates, reminders, announcements, and reflections on daily activities. A class YouTube channel could offer regular video glimpses of teaching and learning. And a live streaming video app like Periscope, which you can set up at a moment's notice, lets others actually watch what's happening in your classroom in real time. The positive implications of the Glass Classroom are broad:

Parents will become more invested in what's happening in class, because they will know precisely what is being taught. This will allow them to ask their children more relevant questions about class activities, support them with their homework, and have a better feel for what you're attempting to accomplish. When you give parents regular, convenient access to the inside of your classroom, you greatly reduce the chance for misunderstanding while building a stronger partnership with some of your most important stakeholders.

Absent students won't fall so far behind. The more "transparent" your activities are from outside your room, the easier it will be for a student who is sick, on a school trip, or removed for disciplinary reasons to access your lessons. Imagine having a student return from an absence without ever needing to ask you for make-up work.

Community members will become more invested in your school. Although local officials and business owners will readily say they support the schools, that idea is pretty abstract when they really don't know much of what happens in those schools. Being able to peek inside will give community members a greater familiarity with your daily activities, building a greater sense of unity in your region and planting seeds for relationships that could result in funding opportunities, shared resources, and a greater overall sense of public pride in the local school system.

Teacher repertoires will grow. Having access to models of others' practice will build teachers' willingness to try new approaches in their own classrooms. This applies not just to the teachers in your own building; if class transparency is extended beyond your school community, your ideas could reach teachers anywhere. If tens of thousands of teachers converted their classrooms to glass, the opportunities for easy, customized teacher professional development would be astounding.

⚙ WHAT YOU CAN DO TOMORROW ⚙

Creating a classroom that allows anyone to look inside takes time. You'll need to educate all stakeholders, build regular sharing into your routine, and learn some new technology. But to get a quick, small taste for what a Glass Classroom is like, try this:

- **Create a social channel for one class.** With your administrator's permission, set up an invitation-only Facebook page or Twitter account for your class (or a single class period if you teach middle or high school). If your school uses a tool like Edmodo, you may already have an online channel that parents and students have access to; this will work fine.

- **Record instruction.** At some point during the day, when you are giving instructions, demonstrating a technique, or otherwise doing something that would be hard to replicate on paper, have someone with a smartphone record you. (Unless you already have permission to record students, just stick to recording yourself this time.) Keep the video short—less than two minutes is ideal. Before you record, explain your purpose to students; build excitement about the idea of being able to see something from class when they are at home that night.

- **Load your video onto your new social channel.** Embed or link the video to your class Facebook page, Twitter feed, or YouTube channel. If you're not sure how to do this, find someone to show you how (your students may be the best resource in this case).

> **Share your channel.** Via e-mail, send parents the web link to the channel, explaining that it contains a video that will give them a glimpse of today's activity and that you are hoping to do more of this in the future. To boost participation right from the start, ask them to add comments or questions to the video post.

A BLUEPRINT FOR FULL IMPLEMENTATION

Step 1: Choose a platform for your social channel.

Before you can start sharing, you need a platform, an online channel from which to share. To build participation and keep yourself from getting overwhelmed, start with just one. Rather than attempting to establish a Facebook page, a Twitter feed, an Instagram account, a YouTube channel, and an Edmodo page, pick one and launch it. You might consider surveying students and their parents to see which platform they use most frequently and start there.

When setting up your social channel, keep in mind that most of these tools offer privacy settings, allowing you to make your channel public or limit its availability to invited guests. How you select privacy settings may depend on what grade level you teach or what your school's Appropriate Use Policy says.

Step 2: Define your content.

When you're getting started, think about what kinds of content you're going to share on a regular basis. Ask yourself a few important questions: Will you post weekly videos of in-class activities as a way to showcase interesting things? A daily written message about the day's activity? Short, practical videos to help students and parents understand assignments? Student reflections?

Talk with students about what they think would be the most useful or interesting kinds of things to share, and how often you should be sharing. Set a tentative schedule and decide who will be responsible for executing those shares—you may want to be in charge at first, but the channel will be more successful if students have ownership and can participate, so keep looking for ways to include them in the operations.

> Set up notifications so you are alerted every time someone adds a new comment or shares anything to your channel.

Step 3: Set guidelines.

What rules should be implemented to ensure your channel is a place where learning is celebrated, rather than a catch-all for useless noise or an unsupervised playground where bullies can take over? Work with students to establish a set of basic guidelines for your channel, agreeing to revisit and revise them as you proceed.

Step 4: Educate stakeholders.

Some administrators and parents may have reservations about using social media in this way. They may be concerned about privacy, cyber-bullying, and safety. You can assuage these concerns with education: Whether you do it through in-person workshops or by creating an online video that explains what you're doing, teach stakeholders about how your chosen platform functions, the privacy settings you have in place, the type of content you're going to share, and the guidelines you and your students have established for its use.

Step 5: Secure permissions.

When sharing student names and images online, it's essential to obtain parents' permission. Your school may already have parents sign a release form for this purpose; if not, be sure to send out your own form before you place student pictures or content on your social channel. If you have a public channel, be sure parents know this, and give them the choice of opting their children out—this means you will need to keep these students off-camera whenever you are recording, and leave their names out of any written shares. Usually, only a few parents will choose this option, but offering it demonstrates courtesy and professionalism, while building a sense of trust.

Step 6: Start sharing.

Your channel will become a vital place for learning only if you use it consistently. Set up a schedule of sharing and stick to it. Whether it's once a day or once a week, consistency is key to getting stakeholders used to seeing your posts. You can give a bigger boost to your channel by promoting it: If it's public, make a concerted effort to invite parents, your colleagues, administrators and community members to view and participate in it. Include links to your channel in newsletters and emails—simple strategies that invite curious readers to engage with your content.

Step 7: Be vigilant.

Even with guidelines in place, you must watch your social channel carefully. Set up notifications so you are alerted every time someone adds a new comment or shares anything to your channel. Be sure to make your own voice heard on a regular basis: When students, parents and administrators see you sharing content and reminding participants about appropriate use, they will feel comfortable that your channel is a useful tool for learning, rather than a dangerous playground.

Step 8: Expand.

Once you and your students are comfortable with a single platform, expand your reach to others: You might join more social media platforms, or just add other features or special opportunities to your existing channel. For example, if your class is going to be participating in a TodaysMeet discussion (a kind of private online "chat room" that anyone with the web address can visit), share a link to the TodaysMeet room with outsiders ahead of time, so they can participate or just observe. Or if you set up a camera to broadcast an event for a Google Hangout on Air (a free video conferencing tool that will show your event live and store a recording of it later on YouTube), you can then share links to the live or recorded event through your main social media channel.

OVERCOMING PUSHBACK

Despite the ubiquity of digital learning tools and the omnipresence of social media, you still might encounter some resistance to using these resources. Here are the most likely objections to setting up a Glass Classroom:

My students aren't old enough for social media accounts. Some platforms have minimum age requirements, which would preclude elementary students from setting up their own accounts. If you want to use these networks, set up an account for the class under your name and share the username and password with students. Alternatively, you could use a social network designed for student use, like Edmodo or Schoology.

Kids are not mature enough to use social media responsibly. Frankly, this can be said about a lot of adults using social media. Digital citizenship is a vital skill set for all people living in this century, so why not teach it in school? If you teach a six year old how to use Twitter or Instagram and these lessons are reinforced throughout the year every year, all students will get it, and they will carry these appropriate practices into their lives outside of school.

Parents are concerned about privacy. From the start, be respectful of these concerns and keep parents in the loop: Share your rationale and vision with parents, educate them about the tools you plan to use, and always obtain written permission before introducing a new level of transparency (see steps 3-5 in the Blueprint for Full Implementation section). And remember, although it limits some of the benefits that can come from a Glass Classroom, your channel *can* be closed to the public: An invitation-only Facebook page can be set up, or an app like Homeroom (gethomeroom.com) can be used to create a private online album of photos and videos, shared only with parents.

I don't want people seeing every single thing that happens in my classroom. You may not be comfortable having your work on display, especially when it comes to video sharing. This discomfort may come from insecurities about imperfections in your teaching, general self-consciousness, or the desire for some privacy in order to bond with your students. Keep in mind that what you share doesn't have to be perfect—you're sharing it to improve understanding and to build community, not to demonstrate your own skills. If you don't love being on camera, stick to sharing student work, or have students take turns being the ones on video. And remember, *you* decide what to share: Unlike a real classroom made of glass, you can put your walls back up anytime you wish.

Parents won't use it. Like everyone else, parents are saturated with digital messages from everywhere and, naturally, it will be a challenge to direct their attention to your classroom's social channel. If you choose a platform parents are already using—like Facebook or Instagram—your channel should be a welcome addition to their current social media habits. Regardless of your chosen platform, you can build parent participation if you share a few high-interest activities at the very beginning to really pull in lots of parents and get them used to seeing great content on your channel. Do the opposite—sharing mundane content on an inconsistent basis—and your channel will indeed be a ghost town.

THE HACK IN ACTION

Starr Sackstein, a high school English and journalism teacher at World Journalism Preparatory School in Flushing, New York, embodies the concept of the Glass Classroom. For several years, she has been sharing her classroom activity online through blog posts and photos. In the fall of 2014 she began documenting a new, student-centered approach to grading through a collection of blog posts and YouTube and Periscope videos. "The authenticity of seeing what a learning space looks like is so valuable," Sackstein says, about sharing her classroom through a social channel. "It's good for my students to be able to show the world the amazing things that they're doing."

With the free Periscope app, Sackstein uses her smartphone to record students at work on various projects and presentations. Sometimes she asks students for feedback about what they're learning, and a live audience can tweet questions that Sackstein or the students can immediately answer. These recordings can be viewed live on any device equipped with Periscope, so parents and other interested parties can watch in real time. Sackstein then saves the recordings and posts them to YouTube, so those who can't attend the live session are able to watch and learn later.

Because Sackstein makes these resources available to anyone who's interested, she gives parents insight into what their children are learning in her class and allows administrators a broader look at her teaching than they'd get from a simple observation. The videos also help co-workers understand exactly what's going on in her classroom, which provides valuable free professional development for teachers at Sackstein's school and all around the world. "Periscope is an opportunity for me to share with others how a student-centered classroom looks and runs. There's a depth, a three-dimensional look at what goes on in my class." In effect, she's created a Glass Classroom.

Many teachers feel that the work we do just isn't fully understood by the outside world. In the past, our ability to showcase that work was limited, but technology now allows us to pull back the curtain and share the fantastic things happening in our classrooms—*really* share them—with all the nuance, complexity, and immediacy a visitor might get from standing right inside our rooms.

THE 360 SPREADSHEET

Collect a Different Kind of Student Data

One sees clearly only with the heart. Anything
essential is invisible to the eyes.
— ANTOINE DE SAINT-EXUPÉRY, *THE LITTLE PRINCE*

THE PROBLEM: TURNING STUDENTS INTO NUMBERS

FOR AT LEAST a decade now, the driving force behind education reform has been data. We talk about collecting data, analyzing data, and making data-driven decisions. All of this data can certainly be useful, helping us notice patterns we might not have seen without aggregating our numbers in some way, looking for gaps and dips and spikes, allowing us to figure out where we are strong and where we need help. In terms of certain academic behaviors, we can quantify student learning to some extent and improve our practice as a result.

And yet, we know this is not enough. We know our students bring with them so many other kinds of data. So many other factors contribute to academic success: the atmosphere in their homes, the demands of their out-of-school school schedule, the physical concerns that distract them, the passions and obsessions that consume them. These things are much harder to measure, so we don't even try, focusing instead on the things we can convert to numbers.

In the spring of 2015, Denver elementary teacher Kyle Schwartz asked her students to complete this sentence in writing: "I wish my teacher knew..." The student responses were so unexpected, so moving, Schwartz shared some of them online, igniting a movement that went viral within hours. Teachers everywhere asked their students the same question, learning in late spring things that had troubled their kids all year:

> "I wish my teacher knew how much I miss my Dad because he got deported to Mexico when I was 3 years old and I haven't seen him in 6 years."

> "I wish my teacher knew that I've been having trouble balancing my homework and sports lately."

> "I wish my teacher knew I don't have pencils at home."

The overwhelming response to this idea illustrates a significant gap in the data we collect on our students. Despite our efforts to carefully examine student performance and choose instructional interventions that best meet their needs, the truth is, we need to be collecting, organizing, and analyzing more robust data on our students—facts about their home lives, their likes and dislikes, their learning preferences—the things that really matter.

THE HACK: COLLECT DATA ON THE WHOLE CHILD

Most teachers make an effort to get to know their students, and many regularly distribute surveys at the start of each school year to speed up that process. The problem is, most teachers read these surveys once, then file them away. Sure, they might have every intention of

Name	Passions	Family	Activities	Academics	Food & Drink	Physical	Skills	Other
Adams, Toby	STL Cardinals Minecraft Skylanders	Lives w/ mom, dad, brothers Jordan (6) and Ben (4), and cat Mooshoo.	Baseball Chess Drawing	Loves Percy Jackson books Hates cursive	Peanut M&Ms Raw oysters!!	Asthma Broke arm last year	Knows a little coding	New to area – moved from Berkeley, CA Scared of dogs
Carter, Jaylen	Minecraft Sharks Martial Arts Jackie Chan	Lives with mom, sister Kayla (3) and dog Reggie.	Tae Kwon Do	Just started to like math last year	BBQ ++ Hates cantaloupe Snickers ++	Left-handed	Cooking omelets and brownies	Loves being outside and roller coasters
Christopher, Tim		Lives w/ mom, at dad's every other wkend. ½ bro Kenny (2) at Dad & stepmom's.				Bee sting allergy		Homeschooled last year
Fong, Jenny	Earrings (just pierced this summer) Ross Lynch	Lives with mom, dad, Sister Lucy (15) and brother Michael (7)	Soccer Gymnastics Sticker collection	Loves to read but doesn't want to be seen carrying big books.	Peaches, grapes, cherries Sour cream & onion chips	Occasional eczema Just started wearing contacts	Braiding hair GREAT with special needs kids	Wants to be a pediatric oncologist when she grows up

Figure 10-1

returning to the surveys and reviewing them later, but far too often, that time never comes. We rely on our day-to-day interactions for relationship building, and although we get to know some students quite well this way, others just fade into the background.

A 360 Spreadsheet is a place for teachers to store and access the "other" data we collect on our students, giving us a more complete, 360-degree view of each student. It's a single chart that organizes it all and lets us see, at a glance, things we might otherwise forget. Many teachers already keep track of students' birthdays. Think of this as a birthday chart on steroids. Figure 10-1 is just one possible version of a 360 Spreadsheet:

Because the 360 Spreadsheet is a single document, teachers can access it much more easily than they could a whole folder of surveys. Having the information formatted this way also makes it immediately clear which students a teacher needs to get to know better.

The chart in Figure 10-1 sorts student information into the following suggested categories:

- **Passions:** What is the student *really* into? Keeping track of things like hobbies, collections, and other hard-to-categorize obsessions will help you connect with your students. This information will boost your ability to help students select books for independent reading, choose topics for writing or research projects, or even better understand math or history concepts by placing them in the context of things they are just crazy about.

- **Family:** The home environment plays a major role in how well a student performs academically. This category can include information about whether a student lives in one home or travels between the homes of two parents. It might ask about the number of people who live in the household. It can also include other family-related facts, like whether anyone at home is dealing with an illness, is currently incarcerated, has special needs, travels frequently, or has a noteworthy profession or skill set (Mom is a circus performer? Probably worth noting.)

- **Activities:** This category will help you better understand what outside activities fill up a student's schedule when they are not in school. Are they on a sports team? Do they have a part-time job? Will they be busier on certain days of the week or at certain times of the year? Not only will this information give you a more complete picture of who your students are, it will build your awareness of the other demands placed on their time.

- **Academics:** Here's where you can put things a standardized test won't tell you about a student's academic needs and preferences: If a student struggles with handwriting, expresses a strong desire to work alone, has a strong interest in a particular subject area, or lights up during certain types of activities, record this information; it will help you individualize instruction later.

- **Food & Drink:** No, you are not a caterer. But why not keep a list of each child's favorite candy or snack? While you're at it, record food allergies on this chart as well—the information is probably in the school paperwork already; might as well add it here.

- **Physical:** Along with conditions that are already listed on students' official paperwork, this category can include others that are not, but are still important, like needing to use the restroom frequently or the tendency to get cold easily.

- **Skills:** Our students bring with them talents and skills we may not even be aware of if we don't ask, so when you find these things out, include them in your chart. Has a student been taking violin lessons for years? Add that. Do they know a lot about dairy farming? Origami? Photography? Put it all in there. Not only will knowing about these skills further develop your knowledge of the student, they may also come in handy when you need help or information about an area where you lack expertise.

- **Other:** This seems like it could be a throw-away category, but making room for miscellaneous information is a good idea. Things like sensitivities to loud noises, religious practices, or random facts about student histories (e.g., "Lived in China") should also be recorded, even if they don't necessarily fit into any broad category.

Although these categories offer vital information, they are just suggestions. Teachers can and should collect whatever information is most relevant to them, information that will help you connect to your students as whole people and build strong relationships with them.

⚙️⚙️ WHAT YOU CAN DO TOMORROW ⚙️⚙️

A 360 Spreadsheet works best if you use and maintain it all year long, but by following these steps, you will immediately get an idea of how powerful it can be at any point in the year:

🔑 **Gather the data.** Have students submit their responses to a short list of questions about themselves (3 or 4 questions). Ask about things you haven't already learned about them—look at the list above and choose a few topics you would like to know more about.

🔑 **Build your spreadsheet.** Create a basic table in Microsoft Word, a spreadsheet in Excel, or just make a rough chart on paper—whatever works best for you to catalog the information in one place. Then record student responses, giving each student their own row and using the columns to record individual responses.

🔑 **Use the data.** Over the next few days, find a way to use at least one fact from each student's row in conversation with them—use a highlighter to mark off every time you use an item. Even though students gave you this information themselves, you'll find that most of them are shocked that you remember!

A BLUEPRINT FOR FULL IMPLEMENTATION

Step 1: Take inventory.

Create a questionnaire or survey for collecting information about students. The ideal time to do this is at the beginning of the school year, but it's never too late. Include questions about the topics suggested earlier, or add your own questions. For very young students, this questionnaire can be sent home for parents to complete.

Step 2: Enter data.

This is what separates this hack from what teachers often do, which is to collect the surveys, read them, then file them. By entering the data into a single chart, you can see student data at a glance.

Step 3: Study your data.

It's a good idea to set aside some time right away to read through each student's information carefully, mark anything that seems noteworthy, and start thinking about how you can use this information in your interactions with students. Also, look for gaps: If some categories are a bit sparse for some students, this is your signal to get to know those students better in those areas. If a student didn't supply a response to a certain question, it could indicate a lack of interest in that topic, or it might mean they are not comfortable sharing anything about it yet. Follow up with the student to see what you can learn.

Step 4: Use your data for weekly planning.

The 360 Spreadsheet only works if you use it, and the best way to make sure you use it is to build it into your weekly planning. Sometimes it will influence instructional decisions: If you are thinking about ways to introduce a lesson, reminding yourself of students' interests can help you better tie your content to the things students care about.

Other times your data will help with relationship building: Skim your chart every week for students you've had some trouble with or who have been especially quiet, and find something to ask each of them about. How is the new puppy doing? Are they looking forward to Rosh Hashanah? What have they been building lately in their Minecraft world? Instead of just intending to connect with students, add these specific conversation starters to your weekly plans and you'll see wonderful results.

Step 5: Keep collecting.

What you want to know about students will evolve from the beginning of the year to the end, so keep collecting information. If one student happens to mention that his family went to Paris last summer, use that day's exit slip to ask students to list places they have traveled with their families, and add this information to your spreadsheet. When a student mentions that her aunt and cousin just moved in with her family, take note—this will change the home dynamic and may impact the student's school performance.

OVERCOMING PUSHBACK

I don't have time to enter all this data. Consider collecting the initial round of information electronically: Creating a Google Form would allow student responses to be placed automatically into a Google spreadsheet, and all of these tools are free. From that point, you could manually add new information to the spreadsheet as the year progresses.

I have too many students / I only have my students for a short time / I teach online. In each of these situations, finding a systematic way to quickly learn about your students is even *more* important than it would be in a small, self-contained, full-year classroom, where it's much easier for teachers to get to know their students well. Regardless of your teaching situation, the better you get at knowing your students as whole people, the better you'll be at teaching them.

Some of this information is private; what if other students see it? Although much of the data you collect may seem innocuous enough—who cares if anyone finds out that Johnny likes peanut M&Ms?—some of the information will be private stuff. Treat your 360 Spreadsheet the same way you'd treat other confidential documents—don't leave it open on your desk (or computer desktop), don't share it whole-cloth with other educators, and keep it private even from your own family members. Do remember, though, that you are legally bound to report instances of child abuse or neglect when you learn about them. In these cases, sharing information with your guidance counselor or administrators would not only be appropriate, but required.

I've tried this, and it doesn't work. If you're already pouring this kind of student information into one central document, fantastic. But if you haven't seen real benefits, it's possible you're not using the spreadsheet to its full potential. Do you look it over on a regular basis? When you notice a gap in student information, do you follow up with that student to learn more about him or her? Could you add a few different questions that would help you get to know your students better? Are you updating your chart throughout the year? You already have a system in place; now see if you can tweak it so it works even better.

THE HACK IN ACTION

Lisa Tremonte, a special education teacher at Apshawa Elementary School in West Milford, New Jersey, began using a 360 Spreadsheet in the fall of 2014. After giving students a survey, she entered their responses into the chart, then stored the spreadsheet in the front of her planning binder, which made it accessible at all times and enabled her to add to it over the school year as she learned more about her students. "In a quick glance," she says, "I can access a wealth of information that really matters about my students. I use it to talk to my students about their lives outside of school when we're saying hello or during lunch and snack time."

Although the spreadsheet does serve an academic purpose, offering ideas when students struggle to come up with topics for writing assignments, its greater value is that it makes students feel seen. "It enables me to ask students direct questions about the sports they play, teams they love, their pets, siblings, and passions," Tremonte says. "When I do, the look on their faces says it all. They know that I listen to them, care about them, and think their lives are important. The chart has given me the tools I need to ensure that each child feels loved, safe, and at home in my classroom every day."

Although education has no silver bullets, building strong relationships with our students comes pretty close. It cuts back on classroom management problems, motivates students to work harder, helps us more effectively differentiate instruction, and generally makes school a better place to be for everyone. The easier you can make it to build those relationships, the more they will pay off for you and your students.

HACK YOUR LEARNING

What's next?

The best solutions are often simple, yet unexpected.
— JULIAN CASABLANCAS, AMERICAN MUSICIAN

OOK NOOKS, MARIGOLDS, quiet zones, and pineapples. These are a few hacky solutions to some important school problems. We'd be the first to acknowledge that we haven't eliminated poverty, ended world hunger, or even figured out how to stop standardized testing (we're working on this one though). What we've done is admittedly very simple.

As we said in the introduction, most of these hacks build on something someone has used or is attempting to implement, perhaps even you. They use assets that in most cases are already available to teachers and administrators. They can be initiated tomorrow and be fully implemented over time by taking steps that require no special skills or additional training.

There is no magic ongoing professional development or major financial backing behind these powerful solutions. As hackers, we've just turned the problems around and viewed them with a different lens, from angles that most people may have overlooked. We have asked "what if" questions, never worrying that someone or something will get in the way of our ideas.

We have many more Hack Learning Series books planned, books that will help you solve other big school problems: assessment, Common Core instruction, and rapport building, to name just a few.

Still, we hope you won't wait for us. We hope you have now become a hacker and that the 10 ideas presented here have helped you understand how to look at resources you already have and use them in a different way, so that the problems we haven't covered here, when viewed with your new hacker mentality, will seem completely solvable.

Now go make something happen.

ABOUT THE AUTHORS

Mark Barnes is a veteran classroom teacher, internationally recognized author and speaker, and creator of the Hack Learning Series for teachers and the Hack Learning mobile app. Mark is the author of six education books, including the critically acclaimed *Role Reversal* (ASCD, 2013) and *Assessment 3.0: How to Throw Out Your Grade Book and Inspire Learning* (Corwin, 2015), which encourages teachers to eliminate traditional grades and build an ongoing conversation about learning. His Facebook group, Teachers Throwing Out Grades, is a growing collection of educators, parents, and students, dedicated to changing the way learning is assessed in classrooms around the world. Mark is the publisher of the popular education blog, *Brilliant or Insane*, named a Top 10 education technology blog by EdTech Magazine. He can be found daily on Twitter @markbarnes19, where his tweets reach more than three million people monthly.

Jennifer Gonzalez is a National Board Certified teacher. Her twelve years of classroom experience include teaching English language arts in middle school and preparing pre-service teachers at the college level. In 2013 she started her blog, Cult of Pedagogy, where she shares effective teaching and assessment practices, curates top-notch educational resources, explores how race and culture intersect with education, and studies the effective use of technology in the classroom. Her writing has appeared on Edutopia, Education Week, MiddleWeb, Brilliant or Insane, and Corkboard Connections. She is the author of *The Teacher's Guide to Tech*, available at teachersguidetotech.com, and the host of *The Cult of Pedagogy Podcast*, available on iTunes. Find her on Twitter at @cultofpedagogy.

PUBLICATIONS

Times 10 is helping all education stakeholders improve every aspect of teaching and learning. We are committed to solving big problems with simple ideas. We bring you content from experts, shared through multiple channels, including books, mobile applications, and an array of social networks. Our mantra is simple: Read it today; fix it tomorrow. Stay in touch with us at HackLearning.org and on the #HackLearning Twitter feed.

CPSIA information can be obtained
at www.ICGtesting.com
Printed in the USA
LVOW03s0210071017

551497LV00001B/4/P